THE GOSPEL REVEALED: GOD'S PLAIN TRUTH

Durrelle Gardner

THE GOSPEL REVEALED: GOD'S PLAIN TRUTH
by Durrelle Gardner

Printed in the United States of America

ISBN 978-1-60791-610-9

www.xulonpress.com

Blessings,
Ovrrelle Gardner

This book is dedicated to everyone who has a God-given desire to study, learn the Bible, establish an intimate relationship with God, and apply His powerful principles to everyday life situations.

Contents

INTRODUCTION

To Learn of Him

This Holy Spirit-inspired publication is intended to aid those who desire to learn the Word of God from a simple and practical perspective—just as God intended. In my personal experience, I've found that most people don't study the Bible because they believe it is too difficult for them to understand. This type of mind-set is not only dangerous—"My people are destroyed for lack of knowledge" (Hos. 4:6a)—but it is also a lie from the adversary to keep us from developing into what God intended us to be.

The Bible says, "Study to shew [show] thyself approved unto God" (2 Tim. 2:15 KJV). If God desires for us to learn of Him, certainly He would not make it close to impossible for us to understand His Word. We must simply get the proper materials and dedicate our time to studying and reading His Word on a daily basis.

Unfortunately, many of us rely upon someone else to tell us what he or she believes God is saying in His Word or even what God is doing in our personal lives. There is nothing wrong with seeking wise counsel. However, we will never grow and mature spiritually if we always have to seek someone else to explain what God is saying. The Bible says,

"He made known His ways unto Moses, His acts to the children of Israel" (Ps. 103:7). Isn't this simply because Moses had a heart for God and spent time with Him, while the children of Israel did not?

God's Word was intended to be simple enough for all of His children to understand. Our Lord and Savior Jesus Christ ministered to men and women who were unlearned (not educated), and they received and understood the gospel. Today we live in the dispensation of grace (age or period that we will have to answer to God's unmerited favor toward us) and the age of information, yet many of us still do not take full advantage of all that is made available to us. Most importantly, we have God's Spirit living inside of us to help us to understand if we just seek Him.

He is our comforter, helper, and teacher (John 14:26). He will give us all we need if we just get started reading and studying now! There is nothing that can prevent us (other than ourselves) from learning the Word of God. Take this opportunity today, and use this book in conjunction with your Bible, and watch the Holy Spirit enlighten your biblical understanding as you grow in God's favor and grace.

This book was written to be a companion to the written Word of God. It is not based on opinion or personal experience. It also emphasizes hermeneutics (using Scripture to interpret Scripture), is very easy to read, and can be understood by just about everyone. I think this book is an excellent tool to help young Christians, new converts, and experienced Christians study, teach, and understand the Bible and also memorize Scripture as they grow spiritually.

This text was written in an easy-to-follow format to encourage serious study on a personal level or in a group setting. It can be of benefit in Sunday school, midweek church study classes, or at home as a family study tool. I pray that the Holy Spirit enlightens you as you study God's awesome revelation of the truth. My friends, I bid you Godspeed.

1

Our Salvation Cannot Be Lost

Our salvation is God's free gift of eternal life in His presence. To truly understand this, we must know the meaning of salvation, eternal life, and grace. God does not take back His free gift of eternal life because one of His children commits sin.

Salvation – "the acutely dynamic act of snatching others by force from serious peril. In its most basic sense, salvation is the saving of a life from death or harm. Scripture, particularly the New Testament, extends salvation to include deliverance from the penalty and power of sin" *(Holman Bible Dictionary).*

Eternal Life – "a person's new and redeemed existence in Jesus Christ, which is granted by God as a gift to all believers. Eternal life refers to the quality or character of our new existence in Christ as well as the unending character of this life. The phrase, *everlasting life,* is found in the Old Testament only once (Dan. 12:2). But the idea of eternal life is implied by the prophets in their pictures of the glorious future promised to God's people. The majority of references to eternal life in the New Testament are oriented to the future. The emphasis, however, is upon the blessed character of the life that will be enjoyed endlessly in the future" *(Nelson's Illustrated Dictionary of the Bible).*

Grace – "favor or kindness shown without regard to the worth or merit of the one who receives it and in spite of what the same person deserves. Grace is one of the key attributes of God. The Lord God is "merciful and gracious, long-suffering, and abounding in goodness and truth" (Ex. 34:6). Therefore, grace is almost always associated with mercy, love, compassion, and patience as the source of help with deliverance from distress" *(Nelson's Illustrated Dictionary of the Bible).*

Many of us mistakenly believe that we can lose our salvation. This is simply a result of false teaching and misinterpretation of Scripture. Many Christians struggle to correctly interpret Scripture because of the lack of quality time that is spent reading and studying the Bible. The more time we spend reading and studying the Bible, the better we will know and understand the ways of God. It is simply impossible to deeply know and understand anyone without spending quality time with the person. Because Moses was the prophet of God who spent quality time with Him, God made known His ways to him.

However, the children of Israel lacked a relationship with God, so they only knew His acts (Ps. 103:7). By studying more we will uncover the awesome character of God overflowing with love and grace. This loving God would never condemn those who have confessed His Son as Savior (Rom. 10:13).

The Lord promised everlasting life to all who believe in Him (John 3:16; 5:24). To say that we can lose our salvation means we don't believe the two aforementioned Scriptures or the numerous others that promise eternal life through faith and confession in Jesus Christ. When we accept Jesus Christ as our Lord and Savior, we are sealed with the Spirit of promise for eternity (2 Cor. 1:21, 22; Eph. 1:13, 14; 4:30). If we can lose our salvation, then we are not recipients of God's grace. Grace is unmerited favor that we can't earn or lose—it is an expression of God's loving character (Eph. 2:8-9).

Simply put, to be able to lose your salvation would mean you never received God's grace. God is unlike man—He does not change (Mal. 3:6; Heb. 13:8; James 1:17). His love for us will not change just because we make bad choices or poor decisions. Sin leads to death, and salvation leads to eternal life (Rom. 6:23). Eternal life with God the Father and His Son Jesus Christ is our heavenly inheritance (1 Pet. 1: 3-5). If we believe sin negates salvation, we have to believe that none of mankind will be able to enter into the kingdom of heaven based on these Scriptures:

1. If God kept account of our sin, whether we were saved or not, no one would make it into His kingdom (Ps. 130:3, 4).
2. Because of our flesh, we will all sin (Rom. 3:23). However, a child of God will not habitually live in sin (Prov. 24:16).
3. The law places all flesh under the penalty (Gal. 3:22-25).
4. The Bible says if we confess our sins, God will forgive us (1 John 1:9). What happens if we forget to confess? Certainly God will not condemn us for being human.

God is far greater than the confusion that clouds our minds. If we continue to seek Him, He will reveal Himself to us just as He did to the prophets of old. He does not show favoritism but accepts and reveals Himself to all who seek Him (Acts 10:34-35). Often times we are misled by those who claim to be of God yet live in a state of habitual sin. These are not children of God but are of Satan. No one who belongs to God lives in a state of habitual sin (1 John 3:4-9). If God thought we were worthy to die for, certainly He would not revoke our salvation because of sin (Rom. 8:1, 32-39). Thank God for His wonderful gift of eternal life to all who confess and believe in His Son.

Meditate on These Scriptures

> "I assure you, most solemnly I tell you, the person whose ears are open to My words (who listens to My message) and believes and trusts in and clings to and relies on Him who sent Me has (possesses now) eternal life, and he does not come into judgment, (does not incur sentence of judgment, will not come under condemnation), but he has already passed over out of death into life. Believe Me when I assure you, most solemnly I tell you, the time is coming and is here now when the dead shall hear the voice of God and those who hear it shall live. For even as the Father has life in Himself and is self-existent, so He has given to the Son to have life in Himself and be self-existent." (John 5:24-27 Amplified Bible)

> "The sheep that are My own hear and listen to My voice; and I know them, and they follow Me. And I give them eternal life, and they shall never lose it or perish throughout the ages. To all eternity they shall never by any means be destroyed. And no one is able to snatch them out of My hand. My Father, Who has given them to Me, is greater and mightier than all else; and no one is able to snatch them out of the

Father's hand. I and the Father are one." (John 10:27-30 Amplified Bible)

Commit to Memory

Romans 6:23: ***For the wages of sin is death, but the gift of God is eternal life in Christ Jesus our Lord.*** **(NKJV)**

2

Are We Just Playing Church?
(Part 1)

To answer this question we need to examine the operation and leadership of the early church and the Great Commission given to us by our Lord and Savior Jesus Christ. Our careful examination of these two elements will teach us what we should and should not be doing as a church and what God expects from us in regard to the commission from Christ to the church. We will begin with the Great Commission.

The Great Commission was the Lord's instructions for the apostles and all Christians. This was not a suggestion; it was a mandate for everyone who confesses Jesus Christ as Savior (Matt. 28:18-20; Mark 16:15-18). To understand this great command, we must know the meaning of the terms *disciple* and *preach.*

- Disciple- "a student, learner, or pupil" *(Nelson's Illustrated Dictionary of the Bible).*
- Preach- "to proclaim God's saving work through Jesus Christ" *(Nelson's Illustrated Dictionary of the Bible).*

The first thing you'll notice in the Great Commission is that the Lord expects us to be well learned in His Word. How can we make disciples of all the nations (various types of people) if we ourselves don't know the Word of God? We must understand God's Word so that we will be fully equipped to teach it to others (2 Tim. 2:15-16). Preaching and teaching the Word of God are synonymous. To preach the Word of God means to explain, interpret, and expound on the meaning and intention of the Scripture. Notice that the gift of pastor is combined with teaching (Eph. 4:11).

God expects us to teach the meaning of the Word as we preach it to the lost and to the children of God. The Lord promises that all who believe in Him will perform signs, wonders, and miraculous healings in His mighty name (Mark 16:17-18) and will not be harmed by anything deadly that they might consume (cf. Luke 10:19). Jesus Christ affirms that He will always be present with those who obey Him. This powerful statement is the promise of indwelling power that comes from the presence of the Holy Spirit (see John 14:15-18).

A commission is defined as "an authorization to perform certain duties or tasks" *(Webster's New World Dictionary)*; it is also defined as a command. By definition the great commission is a command from the Lord to all believers to go out and spread the gospel to people of all walks of life and to teach them the meaning of God's Word. The Lord gives all who believe in Him authority to perform miraculous signs and wonders in His name. This is the meaning of the Great Commission, and it applies to every believer.

Meditate on These Scriptures

"I am the vine, and my Father is the vinedresser. Every branch in me that does not bear fruit He takes away; and every branch that bears fruit He prunes, that it may bear more fruit. You are already clean because of the word that I have spoken to you. Abide in Me, and I in you. As the branch cannot bear fruit of itself, unless it abides in the vine, neither can you, unless you abide in Me." (John 15:1-4 NKJV)

"Enter by the narrow gate; for wide is the gate and broad is the way that leads to destruction, and there are many who go in by it. Because narrow is the gate and difficult is the way which leads to life, and there are few who find it." (Matt. 7:13,14 NKJV)

Commit to Memory

2 Timothy 2:15: ***Study to shew thyself approved unto God, a workman that needeth not to be ashamed, rightly dividing the word of truth.*** **(KJV)**

Are We Just Playing Church?
(Part 2)

Every believer in Jesus Christ must understand the principles of Scripture so that he or she will not be deceived. Unfortunately, many of us are too lazy to take the necessary time to study the Word of God, which is required to equip us to be good witnesses for Jesus Christ. For this reason many of us have gotten lost in what I personally identify as "*the church explosion*"—an era when churches are popping up everywhere you can imagine and are led by men and women who are not chosen by God. In all of these churches, bad doctrine is taught to the unknowing, who blindly follow.

The first stage of enlightenment is the understanding of whom and what the church is, how it should function, and who is the head of the church. This information can't be based on anyone's opinion. It must come directly from the Word Of God! The believers make up the church, and they comprise the body of Jesus Christ (Rom. 12:4-5; 1 Co. 6:19). This doesn't have anything to do with any building, structure, or man-led ministry. The people are the church, not the structure where church takes place. Jesus Christ is in the midst of every gathering in His name when hearts and minds are in accord, whether it takes place in the street, the market, or in your garage (Matt. 18:20).

Jesus Christ formed the church to carry out many functions; however, the primary purposes of the church is to minister the gospel of God to the lost and make disciples of all mankind (Matt. 28:19-20). The church of God should function as a band of servants with its leaders serving as an example for everyone else. The church should more resemble a hospital or outreach center than a concert or show (Acts 2:42-47; 4:32-37). God expects the church to be the example to the world (Matt. 5:13-16) in both character and deed (1 Pet. 2:11-12). God's presence should be evident in every gathering in the Lord's name by revelation of the truth, conviction, healings, and signs and wonders.

Jesus Christ is the head of the church and Him alone. No person, whether it be a bishop, pastor, elder, minister, or deacon, can ever be the head of the church of God (Col. 1:15-18). Unfortunately many give their allegiance to man and not to God. The humility and character of our church leaders should resemble that of our Savior (John 13:3-17; Phil. 2:5-8).

If what we're following doesn't resemble what we find in the Word of God, then it can't be of God. He never changes (Heb. 13:8-9). Let us all begin to seek God in prayer for guidance and the truth so that we won't be destroyed for lack of knowledge (Hos. 4:6).

Meditate On These Scriptures

> "You are the salt of the earth; but if the salt loses its flavor, how shall it be seasoned? It is then good for nothing but to be thrown out and trampled under foot by men.
>
> You are the light of the world. A city that is set on a hill cannot be hidden. Nor do they light a lamp and put it under a basket, but on a lampstand, and it gives

light to all who are in the house. Let your light so shine before men, that they may see your good works and glorify your Father in heaven." (Matt 5: 13-16 NKJV)

All who keep His commandments (who obey His orders and follow His plan, live and continue to live, to stay and) abide in Him, and He in them. They let Christ be a home to them and they are the home of Christ. And by this we know and understand and have the proof the He (really) lives and makes His home in us: by the Holy Spirit Whom He has given us. (1 John 3:24 Amplified Bible)

Commit to Memory

Hebrews 13:8: ***Jesus Christ is the same yesterday, today, and forever*** **(NKJV).**

3

Are We Still Conforming to This World?

The Bible says, “Do not be conformed to this world, but be transformed by the renewing of your mind” (Rom. 12:2a). To be conformed to this world means to be in unity with it or in a lifestyle fashioned after its ways and customs. The household of faith should not resemble the world in any way, shape, or form.

Refraining from questioning the salvation of anyone (only God knows who’s truly saved), it is difficult to believe that some of us are truly of the household of faith because of our inability to deny our flesh and our close relationship with the world. Many of us who claim to belong to Christ are still conforming to the world. The Bible says not to have fellowship with unbelievers (2 Cor. 6:14-18), yet many of us are still aligning ourselves with those who do not believe. In doing so we become partakers of their wicked deeds (2 John 1:10-11). Friends of the world are enemies of God (James 4:4).

I’m not advocating that we alienate ourselves from those who are unsaved—how else would they come to know the Lord without our witness? I’m simply saying that our own testimony comes into question when we align ourselves with those who openly show no regard for God or just don't have decent moral standards. The psalmist said, "I will set no wicked thing before my eyes" (Ps. 101:3), and the Lord said, "If your right eye causes you to sin pluck it out"(Matt. 5:29a). However, many of us view things that we know are offensive to God (TV shows, Internet etc.).

Many of us claim to believe God, but we don't obey His Word. Obedience is following the entire counsel of God (the whole Bible). The world accepts a portion of the Word and neglects to follow the rest. And so do many of us. Jesus said, "If you love Me, keep My commandments" (John 14:15). If we are keeping His commandments those who belong to the world should be extremely uncomfortable when in our company because we are of God and they are of the world – our character should trouble them (John 15:18-20). If those who belong to the world feel comfortable in our presence, something is wrong with our living testimony.

The Bible says if anyone is in Christ, he is a new creation, the old has passed away and all things have become new (2 Cor. 5:17). Our past relationships should change after we've received salvation because we have become new. So why hasn't our character changed? Can we truly be saved and have the same attitude, mind-set, and friends that we had before we accepted Jesus Christ as our Savior? The Bibles says no!

1. No one who has the Holy Spirit living inside sins habitually (1 John 3:4-9).
2. The righteous may fall, but we will not be consumed by sin (Prov. 24:16).
3. Those who claim to be saved but habitually sin must be abandoned if they don't repent (1 Cor. 5:9-13).
4. A lifestyle of right standing before God is proof that we belong to Him (1 John 2:29).

5. Those who openly deny Christ will damage our good character (1 Cor. 15:33).

My friends, do not be deceived, just because you're not stealing, committing adultery, fornicating, or in a homosexual or lesbian relationship doesn't mean you're not sinning against God. If you're living a life of disobedience, you're sinning against God. He hates disobedience (1 Sam. 15:22). Take a moment to examine whether your life is characterized by disobedience to God. If so, ask Jesus Christ to forgive you for your sins and come into your life and be your Lord and Savior (1 John 1:9). Even if you did it before, do it again and mean it in your heart (Rom. 10:9-10, 13).

This chapter is by no means an attempt to drive the children of God off onto an island by themselves away from the rest of the world. This is simply an attempt to reveal to God's children the importance of being a living example of Jesus Christ for all to see. We can't be examples to anyone if we're doing the same things that they're doing or if we are in agreement with their wicked behavior. We must be mindful that we don't have to commit the sin to be guilty—omission is just as bad. We are not expected to leave the world (John 17:13-19) but to be a living example of love, forgiveness, patience, self-control, and faithfulness to God (Matt. 5:13-16).

Meditate on These Scriptures

> For though a righteous man falls seven times, he rises again, but the wicked are brought down by calamity. (Prov. 24:16 NIV)

> There is therefore now no condemnation to those who are in Christ Jesus, who do not walk according to the flesh, but according to the Spirit. For the law of

the Spirit of life in Christ has made me free from the law of sin and death. (Rom. 8:1-2 NKJV)

Commit to Memory

1 John 3:6: ***Whoever abides in Him does not sin. Whoever sins has neither seen Him nor known Him.*** **(NKJV)**

4

As the Battle Grows Fierce, Will We Abandon Our Mission, Or Will We Remain and Stand?

There are a number of things we must understand about the Christian walk if we intend to be successful in fulfilling God's purpose for our lives. Christianity is not a promise of a trouble-free life consisting of singing, rejoicing, and freedom from pains and struggles. It is an existence filled with trials and victories in Jesus Christ our Lord. However, these trials represent the spiritual battles that many of us don't believe exist. The Bible clearly states that we are in a spiritual battle; however, we have been fully equipped with all we need to be successful in our Christian walk and win the spiritual battles that are ahead.

1. We are definitely in a spiritual battle (Eph. 6:12-18).
2. God has a mandate for each of us (Matt. 28:19-20).
3. Because we are followers of Jesus, we have many enemies (John 15:18-19).

4. If you live a Christian life, you will suffer persecution (2 Tim. 3:12).
5. At some point you will have to make the choice to stand for the LORD and penetrate the kingdom of Satan or just be lukewarm (Matt. 6:24; Rev. 3:14-18).
6. The devil desires to destroy all of God's children (1 Pet. 5:8-9)
7. We have all we need to succeed (Luke 10:19; 2 Cor. 10:3-6).

The battle begins the minute we accept Jesus Christ as our Savior. This battle always takes place in our minds. This is why our minds must be renewed with the Word of God if we intend to win this battle against the forces of evil (Rom. 12:2). Following our old way of thinking will always render the same results. The Christian walk is a life of continued trials and testing. This will never change. The more trust God has in us, the more trials He will allow us to encounter. This testing is designed to prepare us to help others and for what is yet to come; however, we must be mindful that we cannot move on until we have successfully completed the last test. Examples of succeeding through trials can be witnessed in Scripture.

1. Joseph remained faithful to God throughout his testing (Gen. 45:3-8).
2. Job never cursed God, although he suffered during his trial (Job 2:7-9).

Our trials will never go away. In fact, the more we impact the lives of people, the more we will suffer trials and testing. We must remain faithful to God during our trials and pray continuously. The more intense our trials become, the more we need to pray and stay focused on the Word of God and not our situation. After we've done all that we can, we must stand firm on the Word of Him whom we believe and trust (Eph. 6:12-18).

Meditate on These Scriptures

> For we do not wrestle against flesh and blood, but against principalities, against powers, against the rulers of darkness of this age, against spiritual host of wickedness in the heavenly places. Therefore take up the whole armor of God, that you may be able to withstand in the evil day, and having done all, to stand. Stand therefore, having girded your waist with truth, having put on the breastplate of righteousness, and having shod your feet with the preparation of the gospel of peace; above all, taking the shield of faith with which you will be able to quench all the fiery darts of the wicked one. And take the helmet of salvation, and the sword of the Spirit, which is the word of God; praying always with all prayer and supplication in the Spirit, being watchful to this end with all perseverance and supplication for all the saints (Eph. 6:12-18, NKJV).

> "Behold, I give you the authority to trample on servants and scorpions, and over all the power of the enemy, and nothing shall by any means hurt you" (Luke 10:19 NKJV).

Commit to Memory

1 Peter 4:17: ***For the time has come for judgment to begin at the house of God; and if it begins with us first, what will be the end of those who do not obey the gospel of God?*** **(NKJV).**

5

Do You Have a Relationship with God?

A relationship can be defined as a bond or union between two or more people. It's not just a mere acquaintance. It is a connection between two or more people driven by love and respect and formulated by spending time together. In regard to God it's built on all of the aforementioned things, with the principle being total reverence. In order to walk in power (live in boldness, confidence, and faith in God), we must have a relationship with Him. Many of us are confused about what it means to have a relationship with God.

The truth of the matter is that having a relationship with God is similar to having a relationship with anyone else, except He demands and deserves reverence. He also deserves our time and attention, just as we give them to our loved ones. These are some examples of how our relationship with God should be.

1. Moses had a personal and intimate relationship with God (Ps. 103:7; Num. 12:1-8).

2. Daniel had a pleasing relationship with God (Dan. 6:7-10; 10:10-12).
3. Jesus gave us an example of a relationship with God (Matt. 14:23; Mark 1:35; 6:46; Luke 5:16; 6:12; 22:41). Prayer is our communication line with God.

A relationship is developed as a result of spending time together. It is simply impossible to have a relationship with someone if we don't spend time with, learning about our differences, likes, and dislikes. Our desire to spend time with God is an indication of whether we truly love Him. Spending time with the Lord means reading the Bible on a daily basis and maintaining a strong prayer life. Reading the Bible is equivalent to fellowshipping with Jesus Christ.

1. Jesus Christ is the Word of God made flesh (John 1:1, 14; Heb. 10:5-7).
2. When we pray, nothing is between God and us (Luke 23:44-45).

If we truly love God, we will desire to spend time with Him and establish a close relationship with Him. If we have no desire to pray daily and study the Bible, that is an indication that we don't have a relationship with God or seeking to establish one. Isn't it ironic how we spend all of our time with someone when we're in love (or lust), and yet we're always too busy to pray and study the Word of God, when He is the most important and valuable part of our lives? Unfortunately many of us just take God for granted and put everything and everyone ahead of Him. We must return to our first love (Rev. 2:1-5)

These are three important principles that we must live by in order to develop or improve our relationship with God. They must be the staples of our lives if we intend on establishing a relationship with God.

1. Pray daily and give thanks to God—this is His will (2 Thess. 5:16-18).
2. Study the Bible to be approved by God and well equipped (2 Tim. 2:15; 3:16-17).
3. Confess our sins daily so God can hear our prayers (1 John 1:9; Psalm 66:18).

Building a relationship with God through prayer, Bible study, and obedience to His Word is the single most important aspect of our Christian walk. It is simply impossible to over emphasize the importance of building an intimate relationship with God. This intimacy is nothing at all like what we're accustomed to in a natural relationship. It is a spiritual bond with the Holy Spirit that enables us to understand the ways and character of the God of the entire universe as we study the Bible. As a result we become sensitive to the things that please and displease Him.

An intimate relationship with God will also prevent us from grieving His Spirit and will build tremendous confidence in our Christian walk. Only through an intimate relationship with Him will we really understand how loving and merciful our heavenly Father truly is. If you don't have a relationship with God, pray daily that He will give you a greater desire to know Him. Start setting aside specific moments throughout your day to be alone with God in prayer without any distractions. Continually seek Him, and soon you will be experience the most fulfilling relationship possible. Nothing can fulfill our lives like God can!

Meditate on These Scriptures

Study and be eager and do your utmost to present yourself to God approved (tested by trial), a workman who has no cause to be ashamed, correctly analyzing and accurately dividing rightfully handling and skillfully teaching the word of truth. (2 Tim. 2:15 Amplified Bible)

Everyone who believes (adheres to, trusts, and relies on the fact) that Jesus is the Christ (the Messiah) is a born-again child of God; and everyone who loves the Father loves the one born of Him (His offspring). By this we come to know (recognize and understand) that we love the children of God: when we love God and obey His commandments (orders, charges) – when we keep His ordinances and are mindful of His precepts and His teachings. (1 John 5:1-2 Amplified Bible)

Commit to Memory

Jeremiah 15:16: ***Your words were found, and I ate them, and your word was to me the joy and rejoicing of my heart; for I am called by your name, O Lord God of hosts.*** **(NKJV)**

6

We Have Freedom in Jesus Christ

Many of us endure all sorts of unnecessary pain and suffering because we have no idea who we are in Jesus Christ. The Bible says, "If anyone is in Christ, he is a new creation; old things have passed away: behold, all things have become new" (2 Cor. 5:17). Once we truly understand this verse, our lives will change forever. Understanding this verse and our relationship with God through Jesus Christ will give us boldness to speak the truth, freedom from our past, and deliverance from church tradition.

To be in Christ means to accept Him in your life as LORD and Savior, to allow Him to have complete dominion over you and all of your affairs, to turn away from your previous way of living and thinking, and to adapt to the principles of Scripture. You are now living a life of total obedience to the written Word of God. This union with God through Jesus Christ gives birth to the new creation (2 Cor. 5:17) that is in you and empowered by the indwelling of the Holy Spirit of promise (John 14:15-17). This powerful relationship with God will give you freedom from old traditions, and destructive, false teaching by enlightening you with the truth (John 8:31-36).

Many of us also live powerless lives because we're still following Old Testament ceremonial laws and traditions. This type of lifestyle diminishes the freedom available to us through Jesus Christ and stunts our spiritual growth. We will not develop and grow spiritually until we accept the full grace of God. This "full grace" means accepting everything that is available to us as born-again Christians. Confessing and believing in Jesus Christ as Lord and Savior means letting go of our opinions and old traditions and walking in His completed work at the cross—which is obedience. Notice these two important principles.

1. God has given us a new and better covenant through Jesus Christ (Heb. 8:7-13). This new covenant set us free from Old Testament laws that we did not have the power to keep.

2. We are living in the dispensation of God's awesome grace (the time period in which we will be held accountable for the unmerited favor and grace God has shown to us). We must always be mindful that this grace did not come cheaply; it was purchased with the blood of Jesus Christ. This awesome grace from our loving heavenly Father gives way to a life free of constant stress and works because He has given us all things (Rom. 8:32-34).

Some of us refuse certain meats because of Old Testament law (Deut. 14:3-20). If a particular meat or food is harmful to our health, we should by all means avoid it, but that is the only reason we should abstain from meats. We should not abstain from any meat because of Old Testament laws. This is what the Bible says about abstaining from meats.

1. The Lord told the apostle Peter that nothing He has cleansed is common (Acts 10:9-15).
2. Strong faith sets us free from tradition (Rom. 14:1-3, 14-17).
3. The prayers and giving of thanks sanctifies our food (1 Tim. 4:1-5).
4. The truth is made clear to all who walk in faith (Titus 1:15-16).

Does God require us to follow traditions, holidays, and festivals? Are any of these celebrations important to God? The answers to these questions are easily found if we observe the entire counsel and character of God. The Bible makes it clear what God desires of us in our Christian walk. This list of important principles will help us to understand exactly what the Bible teaches about holidays, festivals, etc.

1. God desires obedience, not sacrifice (1 Sam. 15:10-22; Matt. 12:1-8).
2. Our desire should be to please and obey God, not man (Col. 2:11-23).
3. The children of God are set free forever through Jesus Christ (John 5:24; 8:31-36).

One of the most debilitating things we can do is continue looking back after we've accepted Jesus Christ into our lives. Holding on to negative images from our past will prevent us from walking in the freedom and grace that God has made available to us. Holding on to positive images from the past can be very helpful; however, we must learn to look ahead and not back.

1. Lot's wife suffered the consequences of holding on to the past (Gen. 19:1-26).

2. We're not ready for service if we can't let go of the past (Luke 9:57-62).
3. Turning back to the past can be devastating to our future (Num. 14:1-38).

Our freedom in Christ is not something we should take for granted or consider lightly. We must always be mindful of our Lord's great sacrifice for us all. Therefore, we must take hold of this awesome grace that God has made available to us through Jesus Christ and consider that we are no longer strangers but members of His family. We have freedom in Christ because of what He did for us and not what we do for Him. We are joint heirs with Christ, adopted into the royal family of the Most High God.

1. We were once strangers, but now He has joined us together with Christ (Eph. 2:1-22).
2. His Spirit leads us because we are His children (Rom. 8:14-17).
3. We are united as a holy nation unto God (1 Pet. 2:1-10).

If we truly understand at this point what it means to have freedom in Christ, we must begin to place our focus on our purpose as followers of the Lord Jesus Christ. Letting go of our past failures and worldly accomplishments, we must press to reach the mark of a much higher calling and purpose in our lives.

1. We must press to meet the mark of His calling (Phil. 3:12-16).
2. We were created to do good works (Eph. 2:10-13).
3. We were saved by grace and called to a holy calling (2 Tim. 1:8-10)

As born-again Christians (John 3:1-21), it is extremely important that we understand our freedom in Jesus Christ. This is by no means an open door to sin or to take a vacation from service. It is however, a glorious opportunity to give praise and honor to our heavenly Father for His loving grace that has set us free from laws that we didn't have the power to keep. He has delivered us from our past, regardless of how bad it was prior to being born again, and from all sorts of traditions made by man. God has liberated us with His Spirit (2 Cor. 3:17-18), and it is expedient that we walk in this freedom.

At the same time, let us always be mindful that moral laws and standards should always be maintained. Even in our freedom, we are required to maintain good moral Christian (Christlike) behavior. We are the living example of Jesus Christ for those who are unsaved.

Meditate on These Scriptures

> See to it that no one takes you captive through hollow and deceptive philosophy, which depends on human tradition and the basic principles of this world rather than on Christ. For in Christ all the fullness of the Deity lives in bodily form, and you have been given fullness in Christ, who is the head over every power and authority (Col. 2: 8-10 NIV).

> It is for freedom that Christ has set us free. Stand firm, then, and do not let yourselves be burdened again by a yoke of slavery. Mark my words! I, Paul, tell you that if you let yourselves be circumcised, Christ will be of no value to you at all. Again I declare to every man who lets himself be circumcised that he is obligated to obey the whole law. You who are trying to be

justified by the law have been alienated from Christ; you have fallen away from grace (Gal. 5:1-5 NIV).

Commit to Memory

2 Corinthians 3:17: ***Now the Lord is the Spirit: and where the Spirit of the Lord is, there is liberty.*** **(NKJV)**

7

Breaking Yokes and Tearing Down Strongholds

To break the yokes and tear down the strongholds in our lives, we must first be willing to admit to ourselves that they truly exist. To deny that these dominating sins exist in our lives when they do is an open invitation for the adversary to control other areas of our lives. It's like a married man or woman who goes out to the club every Friday night, claiming they just like the atmosphere. However, they always come home with another phone number. Such ignorance and selfish pride will destroy us (Prov. 16:18).

Throughout the Bible there are numerous examples of men whose lives were destroyed as a result of falling prey to strongholds in some area of their lives. These true stories were written by men inspired by the Spirit of God to instruct, and teach us what we should and should not do as Christians (I Co. 10:1-14).

1. Saul suffered from a stronghold of pride that led to disobedience and eventually caused him to lose the kingdom to David (1 Sam. 13:7-13; 15:10-28).

2. Solomon was the wisest man ever to live on this earth. But even his great wisdom was no match for the stronghold of lust that the adversary used to control his life and even damage his relationship with God. Solomon's lack of control over this area of his life enabled the devil to lead him into idolatry (1 Kings 3:10-12; 11:1-7).

Both of these men were chosen by God to lead His people; however, because they submitted to the flesh's desires of lust and pride, the devil was able to ultimately destroy their testimony. This is the devil's goal—to destroy our testimony. If he can destroy our testimony, he can weaken our Christian walk. If we allow him to weaken our walk, it will impede God's will for us, slowing us down and making ministry far more difficult than it was intended to be. He wants to use any foothold that he can to develop it into a stronghold.

To confess to ourselves that these sins control us is only the beginning of the process that will set us free. To completely break the chains of bondage, we must confess these sins to the LORD in complete humility and trust Him to set us free from the power of iniquity. We also must take the necessary steps to avoid being placed in situations that are not conducive to our success. We must do our part by identifying people, places, and things that will tempt us. If we know that these things will tempt us, by all means we must avoid them. These are bold steps that are necessary if we truly desire to be set free from strongholds.

1. Our confession to the LORD is the way to forgiveness (1 John 1:9). This is the stage of seeking God's forgiveness for the act of sin.
2. God gave us His solemn promise that He would not allow us to be overtaken by any of our daily struggles if we give them to Him completely (Ps. 55:22). To

cast all our cares upon Him simply means to confess to Him everything in our lives that we cannot control and trust by faith that He will do what He said. If we really, truly believe the Word of God, He will set us free from these chains. But we must take part in this process. These strongholds will not just go away with prayer alone.

3. The wrong choices in our acquaintances will destroy us (1 Kings 11:1-9).

Our Savior promised to give rest to all who are heavily burdened if they yoke up with Him. However, He stipulated that we must learn of Him (Matt. 11:28-30).

1. To break the yokes and tear down the strongholds in our lives, we must remove all ungodly behavior from our lives and submit completely to the Word of God. That means reading and studying the Word of God on a daily (everyday) basis, praying day and night and memorizing Scripture. We must also monitor what we view (Job 31:1; Ps. 101:3).
2. Knowing the Word of God is useless if we don't apply it to our lives. We must learn to be doers of the Word (James 1:22-25).
3. God's Word is the key to freedom (John 8:31-32). By submitting to the Word of God, we allow Him to live through us in the person of His Holy Spirit (John 14:15-18). This process is called "being transformed by the renewing of the mind" (Rom. 12:2). To win the battle against the strongholds in our lives, we must allow this process to take place.

We must be mindful that although the blood of Jesus Christ has saved us, we still live in our natural bodies and will always be subject to attacks by the adversary in our minds and our body. However, because we are children of God, the devil has no power over us and must get permission from God to launch his attacks against us (Job 1:1-13). Once we apply these principles to our lives, we will experience deliverance from the yokes and strongholds that the devil has been using to hold us back from God's purpose for our lives.

Meditate on These Scriptures

> "Keep watching and praying, that you may not enter into temptation; the spirit is willing, but the flesh is weak." (Matt. 26:41 NASB)

> There is therefore now no condemnation to those who are in Christ Jesus, who do not walk according to the flesh, but according to the Spirit. For the law of the Spirit of life in Christ Jesus has made me free from the law of sin and death. For what the law could not do in that it was weak through the flesh, God did by sending His own Son in the likeness of sinful flesh, on account of sin; He condemned sin in the flesh, that the righteous requirements of the law might be fulfilled in us who do not walk according to the flesh but according to the Spirit. (Rom. 8:1-4 NKJV)

Commit to Memory

Psalm 55:22: ***Cast your burden on the LORD, and He shall sustain you; He shall never permit the righteous to be moved.*** **(NKJV)**

8

Experiencing and Surviving Trials
(Part 1)

What are trials and tribulations, and what is the difference between the two?

Trial – "a temptation or an adversity, the enduring of which proves the merit of an individual's faith. For the Christian, to encounter adversity is to undergo a trial in which his faith is proved either true or false before God, the highest judge. Since many positive things come about through such trials, Christians are urged to rejoice at their occurrences (Jas. 1:2; I Pet. 4:13)" *(Nelson's Illustrated Dictionary of the Bible).*

Tribulation – "a great adversity and anguish; intense oppression or persecution. Tribulation is linked to God's process for making the world right again. His Son underwent great suffering, just as His people undergo a great deal of tribulation from the world (Ro. 5:3; Acts 14:22)" *(Nelson's Illustrated Dictionary of the Bible).*

From a biblical standpoint, trials are generally experiences that last for a period and are not a result of punishment or sin (Job 1:6-22). Tribulations from a biblical standpoint are generally a result of sin and bring about the judgment of God (Revelation 11-12).

Why do Christians have to experience trials? Answering the question of trials is not a simple procedure but takes an examination of the early history of man, the intentions and schemes of the adversary, and ultimately the will of God.

1. The fall of mankind was the beginning of the rule of our adversary and the beginning of trials for all mankind (Gen. 3:6, 15, 17).
2. When Satan deceived the first two humans, he usurped authority from Adam, who had been given authority from God over all the earth (Gen 1:26-28).
3. Satan has the title deed to this present world system and intends to use every opportunity to deceive us as he did Adam and Eve (2 Cor. 4:4).
4. Because Satan is in control of this present world system, there are many who follow him and will always be in opposition to the work of the kingdom (1 John 5:19).

God allows trials in our lives because He loves us and wants us to be able to use our experience to comfort others who are suffering the same types of trials. Regardless of how painful or unfair our trials may seem, they are not a form of punishment but are designed specifically for each individual so that he or she may develop and mature spiritually.

1. As joint heirs with Christ, we must share in His suffering (Rom. 8:17).

2. Our trials will enable us to develop patience (James 1:2-4). If we lack patience, God will not be able to use us.
3. God will perfect and strengthen us after we have humbled ourselves and endured suffering through our trials (1 Pet. 5:5-11).

Remember that although Satan is the god of this world system (2 Cor. 4:4), he is only a created being—a fallen angel (Isa. 14:12-15) and must get permission from God to launch his attacks at us (Job 1:6-12). God is ultimately in control!

Meditate On These Scriptures

> Consider it pure joy, my brothers, whenever you face trials of many kinds, because you know that the testing of your faith develops perseverance. Perseverance must finish its work so that you may be mature and complete, not lacking anything. (James 1:2-4 NIV)

> You, however, know all about my teaching, my way of life, my purpose, faith, patience, love, endurance, persecutions, sufferings—what kinds of things happened to me in Antioch, Iconium and Lystra, the persecutions I endured. Yet the LORD rescued me from all of them. In fact, everyone who wants to live a godly life in Christ Jesus will be persecuted. (2 Tim. 3:10-12 NIV)

Commit to Memory

James 4:7: ***Therefore submit to God, resist the devil and he will flee from you.*** **(NKJV)**

Experiencing and Surviving Trials
(Part 2)

What should our response and attitude be in the midst of a trial, and is there a correct way to respond to trials? The correct attitude and response to trials can be found throughout the Bible. We must use these examples as blueprints for surviving trials and maintaining the proper attitude throughout these challenging experiences. These examples provide the keys for surviving our trials.

1. Joseph, the son of Jacob, correctly responded in the midst of his trials (Gen. 37:28; 39:20; 40:13-14, 23; 45:5, 8).
2. Job responded correctly in the midst of horrendous trials only a select few could have survived (Job 1:14-19, 2:7, 9; 13:15).
3. Our Lord and Savior Jesus Christ responded correctly in the midst of the worst trial (separation from the Father) known to mankind (Matt. 26:38-39).

Our response in the midst of a trial is a measure of our spiritual maturity and faith in God. If we can give God praise in the midst of our trials, we are truly growing spiritually.

However, if we complain all the time and blame God whenever we're in a trial, then we are still like little children. We will go through the same trials time and time again until we mature spiritually and respond correctly. It is impossible to overstate the fact that the trials we experience are designed for our good. As a secular example, just think about how much easier it is to get a job once you have experience.

Because we know that God is the author of our trials, we should always respond with faith. This is the most important aspect of surviving our trials—knowing who is instituting our trials. Although the adversary (Satan) may carry out some of the attacks that are launched against us, he is not in control of the situation. It is very important for us to understand that the devil is not permitted to have the ultimate victory over the children of God. The Bible teaches us that he must confer with God in regard to all saints, and the Spirit that resides in the children of God is greater than the adversary or any of his cohorts (fallen angels).

1. Satan cannot take our life (Job 2:6).
2. If we allow Jesus Christ to be Lord of our lives, Satan will have no power over us (John 14:30).

In many cases our trials will involve people who are very close to us and have a profound influence on our lives. Whenever possible, the devil will use our friends and loved ones to make our trials more devastating. He knows if he can use them, our suffering will be intensified.

1. Job's wife suggested he curse God and die, and his friends verbally abused him (Job 2:9; 4; 5; 8; 11).
2. Joseph's own brothers sold him into slavery because of jealousy (Gen 37:28).
3. Those who were closest to the Lord abandoned Him (Matt. 26:55-56, 69-75).

Trials are common to all Christians. We will experience trials as long as we occupy this earth. However, instead of getting frustrated when we encounter a trial, we should take a moment to examine our present situation, seek God in prayer for grace and patience to endure throughout these trying times, and always be mindful that God is in control, regardless of the situation.

Meditate on These Scriptures

> For in the time of trouble He shall hide me in His pavilion; in the secret of His tabernacle He shall hide me; He shall set me high upon a rock. And now my head shall be lifted above my enemies all around me; therefore I will offer sacrifices of joy in His tabernacle; I will sing, yes, I will sing praises to the LORD. (Ps. 27:5-6 NKJV)

> Trust in the LORD, and do good; dwell in the land and feed on His faithfulness. Delight yourself also in the LORD, and He shall give you the desires of your heart. Commit your way to the LORD, trust also in Him, and He shall bring it to pass. He shall bring forth your righteousness as the light, and your justice as the noonday. (Ps. 37:3-6 NIV)

Commit to Memory

Ephesians 6:12: ***For our struggle is not against flesh and blood, but against the rulers, against the authorities, against the powers of this dark world and against the spiritual forces of evil in the heavenly realms.*** **(NIV)**

Experiencing And Surviving Trials (Part 3)

Now that we understand from our previous studies that as Christians we will all endure trials as long as we are occupants of this earth, we must know our defenses and how to use them when experiencing trials. Our first defense against the devil's attacks is faith. We must believe God's Word no matter how severe our trial is. Our faith must remain in our God and His promise of protection, comfort, and provision (Ps. 112:6-7; 125:1-2; John 14:15-18; 16:38; Phil. 4:19). We also must exercise the power of the tongue by speaking the Word of God. Speaking the Word continuously strengthens our souls and our faith.

It is very important to always be mindful that the Word of God is filled with power (Heb. 4:12), and that Jesus Christ spoke the Word when He was being tempted by the enemy after fasting forty days and forty nights (Matt. 4:1-11). These two facts underline the importance of speaking God's Word when facing trials. When facing trials we should also surround ourselves with mature Christians who are able to comfort us and offer wise counsel based on the Word of God. However, we must make sure all advice that we receive is scriptural and not just someone's human logic or personal opinion (Prov. 11:13-14).

Prayer is our communication line to God. It is a very powerful defensive and offensive weapon that is available to all Christians. When we pray we have an opportunity to enter the presence of God with our request and supplications. It will calm and comfort our souls, encourage us like nothing else can, and draw us closer to God. Prayer is also an act of obedience to God (Matt. 26:41; Luke 18:1-8; Phil. 4:6-7). Our praise is also a powerful weapon that should be used when going through a trial. Our praise tells God that we believe Him regardless of our circumstances. This is probably one of the most difficult things for most of us to do. However, it speaks volumes of our faith in God and weakens the effect that the trial has on our emotional and spiritual being (Ps. 50:23; 118:17-19; James 1:2-3; 1 Thess. 5:16-18; Heb. 13:15-16).

Unshakable Faith

Our open confession of trust and belief in the promise of God's protection in the midst of our trials is the power of our faith that will short-circuit any trial that Satan comes against us with. The more we read the Bible and quote the Word out loud, the stronger our faith will grow. The ability to say, "The Lord will never leave me or forsake me," in the midst of our darkest and most trying times is the unshakable faith that God wants all of His children to display in times of trouble (Gen. 22:2-14; Job 1:13-22; 19:25-27; Ps. 27:1-10; Heb. 11:23-40).

There is no formula that will prevent us from having to experience trials or assure us our trials will be shortened. However, these steps are based on principles from the Bible and will aid and comfort us as we go from one trial to another. Continue to believe in God and continue quoting

Scripture no matter how severe your trials may be, and you will develop unshakable faith.

Meditate on These Scriptures

> But without faith it is impossible to please Him, for he who comes to God must believe that He is, and that He is a rewarder of those who diligently seek Him. (Heb. 11:6 NKJV).
>
> Now Faith is the assurance (the confirmation, the title deed) of things we hope for, being the proof of things we do not see and the conviction of their reality—faith perceiving as real fact what is not revealed to the senses. (Heb. 11:1 Amplified Bible)

Commit to Memory

Psalm 50:15: ***Call upon Me in the day of trouble; I will deliver you, and you shall glorify Me.*** **(NKJV)**

Experiencing And Surviving Trials
(Part 4)

The Lord did not leave us incapable but left us a Helper (Holy Spirit) to teach us and bring back to our remembrance everything that He said to us (John 14:26). The Holy Spirit will teach us how to use spiritual weapons to ward off the attacks of the adversary. However, we must study the Word of God if we intend to use our weaponry effectively. The Holy Spirit's ability to bring back the Word to our remembrance is possible only if we have hid His Word in our hearts—we must know the Word of God.

For example, if my doctor tells me I am dying, instead of planning my funeral, I will quote the Word of God: "I shall not die, but live, and declare the works of the LORD" (Ps. 118:17). By all means I will follow the doctor's instructions, but I will believe God even more. This does not mean that because I quoted the Bible I am guaranteed to live a longer life or even experience less pain. It simply means that I believe God's Holy Word, and because it is hidden in my heart, the Holy Spirit is able to bring it back to my remembrance to comfort me. Speaking the Word of God is a very powerful spiritual weapon.

Our spiritual weapons are useless if we allow fear, doubt, disobedience, lust of the flesh, or any other immoral sin to dominate us. These are areas of our lives that we must take control of, especially when we are going through trials. Sin will block our communication line with God, leaving us vulnerable to all sorts of spiritual attacks that will heighten our pain as we go through a trial and can even prolong our period of suffering.

1. Harboring sin in our hearts will close our prayer line to God (Ps. 66:18; Isa. 59:2).
2. The faithless cannot please God, but the faithful He will deliver out of all their troubles (Heb. 11:6,7; Nah. 1:7).
3. Fear is not from God—it indicates a lack of faith. If we believe God, we have nothing to fear (2 Tim. 1:7; Ps. 27:1-6).

Our Savior gives comfort to all who suffer. He is willing and able to alleviate our pain and suffering if we believe in Him. We must be willing to give all our cares to Him because He cares genuinely for us (Ps. 55:22; 1 Pet. 5:6-7; Matt. 11:28-30). Because Jesus Christ took on flesh to pay our sin debt, He understands and can relate to all of our suffering and pain. We serve a God who knows personally what it means and how it feels to suffer (Heb. 2:14-18).

As previously stated, we must always be mindful that God is the architect of every trial a Christian will experience. He designs these experiences specifically for each one of us. Some times it's to get our attention, and other times it may be to reveal a specific area in our lives that needs to change. Ultimately God allows trials in our lives to prepare us for the blessings He has prepared for us and to facilitate our spiritual growth and development.

God is in control, and He has the awesome ability to use trials for our good and His glory.

1. Job's trial was initiated and controlled by God (Job 1:1-12; 2:1-7).
2. Joseph's trial prepared him for a great responsibility (Gen. 37:13-28; 41:1-44; 50:15-21).
3. King Nebuchadnezzar's trial broke his pride and revealed the sovereignty of almighty God (Dan. 4:4-37; see Prov. 16:18).

It is clear to see that all trials ultimately come from God. The devil has no control of our lives and can only attack or tempt us if God allows him. Therefore, instead of crumbling in the midst of a trial, we should draw closer to God through prayer, meditation, and studying His Word. As we draw closer to God, He will reveal to us the reason for our trial. We must use the examples of Job, Joseph, and all of the men and women of God in the Bible to learn how to respond to God when experiencing a trial.

He will never leave us or forsake us; and when we come through, we will look back on our trials and give praise to Almighty God for enabling us to mature as a result of these experiences.

Meditate on These Scriptures

> Then Job arose, tore his robe, and shaved his head; and he fell to the ground and worshiped. And he said, "Naked I came from my mother's womb, and naked shall I return there. The LORD gave, and the LORD has taken away; blessed be the name of the LORD." In all this, Job did not sin nor charge God with wrong. (Job 1:20-22 NKJV)

"Now when you hear the sound of the horn, flute, zither, lyre, harp, pipes and all kinds of music, if you are ready to fall down and worship the image I made, very good. But if you do not worship it, you will be thrown immediately into a blazing furnace. Then what god will be able to rescue you from my hand?" Shadrach, Meshach and Abednego replied to the king, "O Nebuchadnezzar, we do not need to defend ourselves before you in this matter. If we are thrown into the blazing furnace, the God we serve is able to save us from it, and He will rescue us from your hand, O king. But even if He does not, we want you to know, O king, that we will not serve your gods or worship the image of gold you have set up." (Dan. 3:15-18 NIV)

Commit to Memory

Job 13:15: ***"Though He slay me, yet will I trust in Him. Even so, I will defend my own ways before Him."*** **(NKJV)**

Experiencing And Surviving Trials
(Part 5)

Our last defense in times of trial can be found in Ephesians 6:10-18. The full armor of God can be identified as the believers' last defense. In Ephesians 6:10 the apostle Paul encourages us to be strong in the Lord and in His might, not our own. This awesome power that Paul refers to is available to every Christian through the Spirit of God. This is not natural might but a powerful force fueled by our faith and obedience.

In the phrase "power of His might," the Greek word for "power" is *kratos*, which means "force, strength, might, more especially 'manifested power,' is derived from a root which means 'to perfect, to complete'; creator is probably connected. It signifies dominion and is rendered frequently in doxologies, I Pet. 4:11; 5:11; Jude 1:25; and Rev. 1: 6" *(The New Strong's Expanded Dictionary of Bible Words).*

In Ephesians 6:11 the apostle Paul advises the church to put on the whole armor of God and immediately explains why—that they may be able to stand against the wiles (schemes, trickery) of the devil. Maybe the reason many of us are not growing is because we refuse to believe that God's Word really works. The fact that Paul tells us to put on God's armor implies its importance. The need for this armor would imply that we are in a battle. Paul often spoke of saints as soldiers fighting in a war. In one of Paul's last letters he stated, "I have fought the good fight, I have finished the race" (2 Tim. 4:7). Paul points to the spiritual battle.

1. Paul confirms that Timothy was called to fight the good fight (1 Tim. 1:18).
2. Paul emphasizes the seriousness of the spiritual battle (2 Tim. 2:3,4).

In Ephesians 6:12 Paul reminds us that our battle is not personal and it's not against natural forces—it's spiritual. Although we may contend with natural flesh, our battle is against spiritual forces. Satan is a spirit being (fallen angel); he must use natural beings and situations to deter and come against us. He is the god of this world system (2 Cor. 4:4), so he has plenty at his disposal. He will use all of his forces to succeed (1 John 5:19). Instead of taking it personally when he uses someone we know to attack us, we must always remember that our battle is against spiritual forces, not the individual. The Word of God is always available to us for help.

1. The battle is the LORD'S—even in our trials (1 Sam. 17:47).
2. If the Spirit lives in us, we will be victorious (1 John 4:4).

In Ephesians 6:13 the apostle emphasizes again the importance of putting on the whole armor of God so that we will be able to withstand in the evil day. This verse assures us that after we have put on the whole armor of God, we will be ready to resist the schemes and temptations of the adversary in the height of our trials. Here are some ways that the whole armor of God will enable us to withstand (or resist) the enemy's schemes and temptation.

1. God's armor will build humility, faith, and patience (1 Pet. 5:6-10).
2. If we subject ourselves to God's commands, the devil will be forced to leave (James 4:7).

In Ephesians 6:14 the apostle Paul tells us to stand confident in our integrity and faithfulness to God. The belt of truth represents the character of a true believer in God. Buckling on the belt of truth represents our confidence as we live the Christian life openly. This confidence comes from following the truth, for obedience leads to freedom (John 8:32; 2 Cor. 3:17). The breastplate of righteousness is the righteousness that we receive through faith in Jesus Christ (1 Cor.1:30). This enables us to live in righteousness (right standing with God). The breastplate is designed to protect our hearts (emotions) from the fiery darts of the adversary.

That adversary will always use people who are close to us by causing them to say or do (unknowingly) painful and hurtful things (cf. Job's wife and friends, Joseph's brothers, and the disciples of Jesus). However, we must always be mindful that it's never personal (Eph. 6:12); it's always spiritual and is never an attack from the individual (Matt. 16:21-23).

Ephesians 6:15 refers to our preparedness after we have properly deciphered and accepted the gospel of God (2 Tim. 2:15). As a result of our preparedness, we are fully confident in the power of Christ Jesus (Prov. 3:26). We have peace and assuredness in our Lord and Savior Jesus Christ and His promises of provision and protection

In Ephesians 6:16 we're advised that above all (most importantly) to take the shield of faith. Faith is the most essential aspect in the Christian walk (Heb. 11:6). It is our faith in our Lord and Savior Jesus Christ that fuels the power in God's armor (Matt. 17:20; Luke 17:6). Our faith is the shield that will protect us from all the fiery attacks that will inevitably be launched against us from the adversary.

Ephesians 6:17a points to the promise of eternal security that comforts the minds of all Christians. The helmet of salvation is the promise of eternal life with God the Father and our Lord Jesus Christ to those who have confessed and believe that Jesus Christ is Lord. It is the assurance from God that no matter what attack Satan launches in our minds, we know that we are sealed with the Holy Spirit (1 John 5:4; 2 Cor. 1:22). We must be mindful that the battlefield is always in the mind. We must always practice rejecting thoughts that are not of or from God. This is possible for all of God's children (1 Cor. 2:16).

No matter what kinds of thoughts Satan projects into our minds, we must always remember that Christ died for all of our sins (Rom. 8:1). We should reject every wicked thought that doesn't glorify God. And don't worry about the situation if you believe in God and have done all that God requires of you (Luke 12:25-31). In Ephesians 6:17b Paul describes the Word of God as a sword. The sword of the Spirit is an offensive weapon (Heb. 4:12) and the most powerful weapon available to God's children when combined with faith (Matt. 17:20). The power of the Word of God is unmatchable and cannot be resisted by the enemy (Matt. 4:10-11). We are to use the Word of God in every situation. How important it is that we learn and quote Scripture.

In Ephesians 6:18 the apostle Paul reminds us to be alert and pray in the Spirit for all of the saints. As Christians and soldiers of the army of the LORD, we must keep in mind those who are in need of prayer—and everyone is in need of constant prayer. It's not enough to just pray for our loved ones and ourselves; we also must pray for leaders, the poor, sick, afflicted, and those being held captive by the adversary, for indeed the adversary holds captive everyone who is unsaved. When we are living in obedience to God, our prayers are extremely powerful (1 Tim. 2:1-4; James 5:13-18). Prayer is essential (Matt. 24:16).

A Prayer for God's Armor

Father God, I come humbled before your presence in the name of my Lord and Savior Jesus Christ. I ask forgiveness for anything that may reside in my heart that's not from you. I ask, Father, that you would create in me a clean heart, and renew a right spirit within me. In obedience to your Word, Father, I put on your full armor. I take the belt of truth and buckle it tightly around my waist, and I take the breastplate of righteousness and put it in place so that I walk upright before you at all times and stand confident and prepared to share the gospel of peace. In addition to this, I take the shield of faith, which is complete trust in your Word, so I'll be able to stand up against the fiery darts of the adversary.

I take the helmet of salvation, which is your promise of eternal life through Jesus Christ, and press it tightly upon my head so that I'll be mindful at all times that the battlefield is in the mind and so that I will receive no thought that is not of God. And I take the sword of the Spirit, which is your Holy Word and an offensive weapon, and use it to combat the attacks of the adversary; and I'll always be mindful to pray for all of the saints. Amen.

Remember to always give praise and thanks to God for all things – even in the midst of your most severe trials. Read 1 Thessalonians 5:16-18 every morning as soon as you awake.

Meditate on These Scriptures

Behold, I have created the blacksmith who blows the coals in the fire, who brings forth an instrument for his work; and I have created the spoiler to destroy. No weapon formed against you shall prosper, and every tongue which rises against you in judgment you shall condemn. This is the heritage of the servants of the LORD, and their righteousness is from Me, says the LORD. (Isa. 54:17 NKJV)

Endure hardship as discipline; God is treating you as sons. For what son is not disciplined by his father? If you are not disciplined (and everyone undergoes discipline), then you are illegitimate children and not true sons. (Heb. 12:7-8 NIV)

Commit to Memory

Ephesians 6:11: ***Put on the whole armor of God, that you may be able to stand against the wiles of the devil.*** **(NKJV)**

9

Generational Curses (Part 1)

What is a generational curse? A generational curse is believed to be an evil (vice or habit) that is passed from one generation of a particular family to another as a result of some sort of sin. This curse is usually in some form of bondage—drugs, alcohol, sex, anger, an unforgiving heart, self-hatred, etc. The belief that many suffer from generational curses probably derived from the Old Testament. Here are a few examples of Scriptures that many of us pick out without examining the entire counsel of God. Attempting to interpret Scripture this way is dangerous.

1. The fathers' sins visiting the sons for generations (Exod. 20:5; 34:6-7).
2. The descendants of the wicked suffering the consequences of their fathers (Ps. 37:28).

However, the argument over the reality of generational curses has been going on for generations and must be examined fully to get the proper understanding of why certain sins are carried from one generation of a family to another. Scripture contradicts the idea of children paying the price for their parents' or grandparents' sins. We also must be mindful that we are living in the dispensation of grace (Eph. 2:8). Because of God's grace and loving-kindness toward us, He will not hold us accountable for anyone else's sins.

1. We will pay the penalty for our own sins (Deut. 24:16).
2. The sins of the parents will no longer be carried to the next generation (Jer. 31:29-30).
3. The righteous will not suffer because of the wicked (Ezek. 18:1-20).
4. We will all reap our own harvest (Gal. 6:7-8).

So now that we know that there are no generational curses, why do certain sins seem to travel from one generation to another? To answer this question, we must examine two very important Scriptures (Prov. 18:21; 23:7).

1. Proverbs 18:21 suggests that many of these so-called generational curses are imputed upon us as a result of what is said or done to us by those who have charge over our lives when we are very young. What we experience when we are in an impressionable stage of life (physical abuse, emotional abuse, etc.) will always have a profound effect on the latter stage of our lives—until the Spirit of God releases us.

2. Proverbs 23:7 indicates that most of these sins (so-called generational curses) and our failures are a result of a negative view that we have of ourselves. These personal opinions or views that we have of ourselves are usually a result of what we have learned or been told by others and accepted as truth. This information

> can come from family, friends, teachers, coaches, etc. When those we love and respect make negative comments to us on a regular basis–certainly when we are at an impressionable age, we will develop deep, internal scars that are difficult to remove.

As parents our actions and decisions have a direct effect on our children (Dan. 6:24; Prov. 22:6). In fact, if we examine Old Testament Scripture, we will find that most of the Israelite kings who sinned against God followed in the footsteps of their fathers and even their mothers (2 Chronicles 21-22). But the point is that these sins are not generational curses. They are all learned behaviors. And these learned behaviors will dominate our lives if we don't first admit that they exist and then ask God for His grace to remove them. Once they begin to dominate our lives, they become strongholds.

If we still believe that these so-called generational curses exist, in a sense we deny the grace of God. Grace can't exist if we are forced to pay the penalty for sins we haven't committed. We're all born into sin, but once we've accepted Jesus Christ as our Savior, we are new creations in Him (2 Cor. 5:17).

Meditate on These Scriptures

> The word of the LORD came to me again, saying, "What do you mean when you use this proverb concerning the land of Israel, saying: 'The fathers have eaten sour grapes, and the children's teeth are set on edge'? As I live," says the LORD GOD, "you shall no longer use this proverb in Israel." (Ezek. 18:1-3 NKJV)

> God "will give to each person according to what he has done." To those who by persistence in doing

good seek glory, honor and immortality, He will give eternal life. But for those who are self-seeking and who reject the truth and follow evil, there will be wrath and anger. There will be trouble and distress for every human being who does evil: first for the Jew, then for the Gentile; but glory, honor and peace for everyone who does good: first for the Jew, then for the Gentile. For God does not show favoritism. (Rom. 2:6-11 NIV)

Commit to Memory

Ezekiel 18:4: ***"For every living soul belongs to Me, the father as well as the son—both alike belong to Me. The soul who sins is the one who will die."*** **(NIV)**

Generational Curses
(Part 2)

Adopted and Learned Sinful Behavior

All of our behaviors are learned or adopted from observation of others. Most of these learned behaviors are sinful because they are taught from the aspect of the natural mind-set. Because we are born and shaped in sin from birth, nothing that we have to offer is of any value in the spiritual world (Ps. 51:5; John 3:3-5). This is why many of these behaviors are sinful. Although much of what we learned was taught to us with good intentions, it was not biblical, so it was sin.

These sins are like seeds and will grow and eventually dominate our lives if they are not turned over to God. By underestimating the power and dominance of these sins in our lives, we actually feed them and enable them to grow from footholds to strongholds (e.g., alcoholics, sex addicts, gamblers, pedophiles, and liars). We have a tendency to hold on to these behaviors because we think we can control them. This is how they grow and become overwhelming.

1. By allowing anger and quarrels to fester, we give ammunition to Satan (Eph. 4:26-27).

2. Attempting to break yokes without God's help develops strongholds (Luke 11:26).

What Are Yokes, Footholds, and Strongholds? And How Do They Operate?

Yoke – A yoke is an apparatus used to join together two animals. Similarly, in the spiritual sense, a yoke is the beginning stage of some sort of sin that we become attached to—lust, drugs, alcohol, prejudice, crime, etc. If not broken these yokes become footholds and eventually strongholds (Matt. 6:14-15.).

Foothold – In some New Testament translations, a foothold is called "place," meaning ground, opportunity, or an open door. The Webster's Dictionary defines it as a secure position *(Webster's New World Dictionary and Thesaurus)*. A spiritual foothold is the beginning stage of total dominance by some sort of sin (Eph. 4:26-27).

Stronghold – A stronghold implies that someone or something is firmly held or controlled by someone else. This is the goal of the adversary. If he gets a stronghold on your life through any form of sin, he will control that area of your life, eventually destroying your testimony. He also will attempt to use you as a pawn to destroy the lives of others (John 10:10). Only Jesus Christ can break such a stronghold (Isa. 9:4-6).

We must always be mindful that a particular area of sin in our life is a yoke when we adopt it, but it becomes a stronghold when it adopts us. If we yield ourselves to strongholds of iniquity, we will become slaves to sin (Rom. 6:16).

Meditate on These Scriptures

"The soul who sins shall die. The son shall not bear the guilt of the father, nor the father bear the guilt of the son. The righteousness of the righteous shall be upon himself, and the wickedness of the wicked shall be upon himself. But if a wicked man turns from all his sins which he has committed, keeps all My statutes, and does what is lawful and right, he shall surely live; he shall not die." (Ezek. 18:20-21 NKJV)

Then Peter began to speak: "I now realize how true it is that God does not show favoritism but accepts men from every nation who fear Him and do what is right." (Acts 10:34-35 NIV)

Commit to Memory

Psalm 1:1-2: ***Blessed is the man who walks not in the counsel of the ungodly, nor stands in the path of sinners, nor sits in the seat of the scornful; but his delight is in the law of the LORD, and in His law he meditates day and night.*** **(NKJV)**

10

Resisting the Enemy

If someone asked you if you were resisting the enemy, what would your answer be? Certainly most of us would say yes, but are we really resisting him? Or are we allowing our flesh to give place to the enemy? If we're continually falling in the same areas of our lives we are not resisting. To resist means to withstand, oppose, or fend off something or someone. To resist the enemy, we must take control of our flesh by resisting its desires to take authority over our actions. Although this is certainly possible, it is not easy. We must learn to place the sinful desires of the flesh under subjection to the commands of God and not pleasure.

Many of these desires come from our old nature prior to being saved. Even after accepting Jesus Christ as our Lord and Savior, we will continue to struggle with the desires of the flesh. These struggles will continue as long as we occupy our natural bodies. To fully understand these struggles and how to resist the enemy's attacks on our flesh, we must observe what the Bible says about the sinful nature of the flesh.

1. The flesh is in opposition to the Spirit (Gal. 5:17-21).

2. Our flesh wrestles with the Spirit for control over our bodies (Rom. 7:13-25).
3. The nature of the flesh is to gravitate to the world (1 John 2:16-17).
4. The desires of our flesh cause temptations and lead to death (James 1:13-15).

The Bible says, "Be subject to God, resist the devil and he will flee" (James 4:7). All Christians must understand the meaning of this powerful statement to live victoriously. If this is a means of vanquishing our greatest enemy—even if it is just for a season—we must understand what it means. Being subject to God means submitting ourselves to every command of God written in Scripture, no matter how difficult. Resisting Satan means refusing to give in to the temptations he imposes on us to destroy our testimony and our lives. If we succeed in these challenges, the devil will have to leave us for a season (Luke 4:12-13). Here are the keys to success.

- **Prayer** – our spirit is strengthened when we pray (Matt. 26:41; Mark 11:24).
- **Faith** – believing God's Word for your life (Luke 10:19; Heb. 11:6).
- **Action** – living a life of total obedience to God (Gal. 5:16; 1 John 2:6).
- **Speaking the Word of God** – to every situation (Matt. 4:1-10; Mark 11:22-23).
- **Forgiveness** – If you do not forgive those who offend you, God will not forgive your trespasses (Matt. 6:14-15; Mark 11:25-26).

To resist the enemy means to deny our flesh and its carnal desires. The first step in this process is examining our lives for any habits or vices that are contrary to the character of Jesus Christ. With each one we identify, we must take them to the LORD in prayer and believe His promise of deliverance (Ps. 55:22). Remember, if Christ lives in you, Satan has no part in you (John 14:30). If we allow anything that is related to this present world system to dominate us on a daily basis, then we are not resisting the enemy. If you fall, repent and continue to serve God; but remember that the righteous will not continuously commit the same offenses (1 John 3:6).

Meditate on These Scriptures

> Be self-controlled and alert. Your enemy the devil prowls around like a roaring lion looking for someone to devour. Resist him, standing firm in the faith, because you know that your brothers throughout the world are undergoing the same kind of sufferings (1 Pet. 5:8-9 NIV).

> Therefore submit to God. Resist the devil and he will flee from you. Draw near to God and He will draw near to you. Cleanse your hands, you sinners; and purify your hearts, you double-minded. Lament and mourn and weep! Let your laughter be turned to mourning and your joy to gloom. Humble yourselves in the sight of the Lord, and He will lift you up (James 4:7-9 NKJV).

Commit to Memory

1 Peter 5:9: ***Resist him, standing firm in the faith, because you know that your brothers throughout the world are undergoing the same kind of sufferings.*** **(NIV)**

11

The Enemies of God's Children

(Part 1)

As children of the Most High God and ambassadors of our Lord and Savior Jesus Christ, we must understand that our Christian walk is a battle. We are in a battle against three very real and very formidable foes. Everyone knows that the devil seeks to kill and destroy each of us (John 10:10). He is no stranger to anyone. However, our flesh and this present world system are just as seducing and destructive as the adversary himself. In fact, our own flesh is probably our greatest enemy. If we can control our flesh and its sinful desires, we will be victorious in every spiritual battle we encounter. These are our enemies.

1. The flesh wars against the Spirit (Gal. 5:17).
2. The world is wicked, ruled by Satan, and adverse to God (2 Cor. 4:4; 1 John 2:16, 5:19).
3. The devil desires to destroy those who belong to God (John 10:10; 1 Pet. 5:8).

Most of us are not effective at all in the struggle against the enemies of God and His children because we don't take into account the seriousness of this great battle that takes place in our lives on a daily basis. On numerous occasions the Bible refers to the Christian as a soldier and his/her walk as a fight. The apostle Paul tells his disciple Timothy about the seriousness of the call of the Lord's followers and the importance of separating themselves from the concerns of this world. This is what Paul says about the spiritual battle.

1. Paul advises Timothy to serve as a good soldier (2 Tim. 2:3).
2. Paul confirms his own fight, victory, and reward (2 Tim. 4:7-8).
3. The servant of God must take his/her walk seriously (2 Tim 2:4-5).

Now that we are aware of who our enemies are, we must study their methods of operation to learn how we can protect ourselves from being controlled or destroyed by these powerful forces. To really comprehend how they operate and the weapons given to us by God to protect ourselves and distinguish these foes, we must examine each one separately.

Flesh – "the physical bodies of humans or animals. In an even stronger sense, flesh is the earthly part of a man, representing lust and desires" *(Nelson's Illustrated Dictionary of the Bible).*

Our flesh can be described as our alter ego. We are like someone with two distinct personalities, one good and one bad. The bad personality would represent our flesh; the good would represent the Spirit of God who lives in us. The flesh operates on our senses, sensualities, and emotions. Its desire is to fulfill its cravings regardless of the consequences.

1. The flesh is powerful and wants control (Rom. 7:14-23).
2. A life led by the flesh is a life of disobedience and self-fulfillment (Eph. 2:1-3).
3. The works of the flesh are sinful (Gal. 5:19-21).

Often we blame the devil for our hardships and misfortunes, but the Bible clearly states that we are destroyed because of a lack of knowledge (Hos. 4:6). Our lack of a good understanding of our flesh will destroy us. Our inability to control our flesh can cause us to make devastating mistakes. With every temptation God makes a way for us to escape (1 Cor. 10:13). Let Joseph be our example in handling temptation (Gen. 39:7-14). We must learn to use these important keys to control our flesh and resist temptations.

1. Monitor what we listen to and what we allow ourselves to watch. Whatever goes into our ear gates and eye gates will affect our thinking and eventually give birth to some sort of reaction (Ps. 101:3; cf. David and Bathsheba).

2. Don't give large amounts of your time to anything that is attached to the world (TV, radio, gossip, malls, or lustful and covetous imaginations). Remember whose servant you are (Rom. 6:16, 22).

3. Have no fellowship with unbelievers (2 Cor. 6:14). Anyone we encounter who does not accept Jesus Christ as Lord is an anti-Christ (1 John 1:18, 22, 23). If we continue to fellowship with these people, we ourselves will eventually be tempted and led astray (1 Cor. 15:33). Remember, God always told the children of Israel not to have fellowship with His enemies (even Solomon failed in this area of his life).

4. Finally, we must begin to spend more time reading and studying the Bible and less time doing the things of the world. God knows exactly what we are doing (Heb. 4:13). If we claim to be saved and we don't spend any time with God in prayer and study, we are only fooling ourselves. God expects more than two minutes of prayer before you go to bed and more than a few minutes a day of reading the Bible. If this is what you're doing, you are fooling yourself and not God (Gal. 6:7).

If we're doing all of these things, then we are walking in the Spirit and we will be victorious over our flesh (Gal. 5:16). We must be mindful that those who know that we are Christians will always be watching us to see if we really believe what we say. The unbeliever is always waiting for an opportunity to point out contradictions in our character. Regardless of what they may say or do, God always expects us to be His ambassadors.

Meditate on These Scriptures:

> So I say, live by the Spirit, and you will not gratify the desires of the sinful nature. For the sinful nature desires what is contrary to the Spirit, and the Spirit what is contrary to the sinful nature. They are in conflict with each other, so you do not do what you want. But if you are led by the Spirit, you are not under the law. (Gal. 5:16-18 NIV)

> We know that anyone born of God does not continue to sin; the one who was born of God keeps him safe, and the evil one cannot harm him. We know that we are children of God, and the whole world is under the control of the evil one. (1 John 5:18-19 NIV)

Commit to Memory

1 John 5:7: ***For there are three that bear witness in heaven: the Father, the Word, and the Holy Spirit; and these three are one.*** **(NKJV)**

The Enemies of God's Children
(Part 2)

"The term 'world' denotes the condition of human affairs, with man alienated from and opposed to God. Jesus wants His followers to live in the world to serve and to witness but not get caught up in the godless pleasures and perversities of life" *(Holman Bible Dictionary)*. The world can be defined as a temporal place of existence for all mankind since no one will exist on this present earth forever. This world, or "worlds system," is an enemy to all of God's children.

1. The world hates the Lord's followers (John 15:18-19).
2. This world is our enemy because Satan is its ruler (1 John 5:19).
3. Satan casts a delusion over the minds of the lost (2 Cor. 4:4).

Because Satan rules this world, almost everything it produces is wicked. From entertainment to government, everything is corrupt. Most of the leaders of this age have designed systems to corrupt the morals of all mankind (TV, movies, video games, Internet porn, and all of the world's delicacies). Everything has become commonplace, from homosexuality to women wearing extremely suggestive and provocative clothing to work on a daily basis, and even in the house of the Lord (church).

1. God prohibits homosexuality (Lev. 18:22; 1 Cor. 6:9 NKJV); the world promotes it (Rom. 1:20-32).
2. God said, "Be holy for I am Holy " (1 Pet. 1:16); the world says, "Fulfill your desires" (Eph 2:2-3).
3. The Bible says not to view wickedness (Ps. 101:3); the world says, "That's entertainment."
4. The Bible says that those who practice wickedness will perish (1 Cor. 6:9); but many of our government officials are pushing for same-sex marriages (while they themselves often times are having extramarital affairs). Satan has even planted his own churches headed by homosexuals and lesbians, and most of the world applauds them.

The Lord knows the dangers of His people getting entangled with this wicked world. For this reason He warned us numerous times to separate ourselves from the world and its wicked system.

1. He warns us to separate ourselves from the world (2 Cor. 6:17)—*Present*
2. God told Israel to separate from the wicked and unclean (Isa. 52:11)—*Past*
3. Even in the very last days, God is still warning His people (Rev. 18:4-5)—*Future*

The Lord knows the dangers of allowing anything to take His place in your heart. That's why He plainly stated, "Where your treasure is, there will your heart be also" (Matt. 6:21). We can identify where our heart is according to our level of commitment to God. Do we seek after the things of the world or the things of God? If we're seeking after God, the majority of our time should be focused on the things of God and not of this world.

If you are giving most of your time to the things of this world, you are part of its system. This means God's love is not in you.

1. If we love this world, we don't have God's love in us (1 John 2:15).
2. Friendship with the world means separation from God (James 4:4).
3. The perfect will of God is separation from the world (Rom. 12:2).

We should not be partakers of this world because this is not our home (Phil. 3:20). We are a part of this world because we are still flesh and blood; however, God expects us to be salt and light to this darkened world (Matt. 5:13-14). This means we should not allow the world to dictate how we dress, what we watch or listen to, or even how we raise our children. It's plain to see that this world's system is designed to destroy our character and relationship with God. We must begin to separate ourselves from this world by giving more of ourselves to God and the things of God rather than the things of this present world.

Begin to spend more time in prayer and Bible study and less time in the world's affairs. This is the only way to defeat this great enemy of God's children. We cannot just leave this world because we are to be salt and light here. However, we must not practice the same behavior as the wicked. We must allow our light to shine by being the best Christian example we can possibly be—even if it is unpopular.

Meditate on These Scriptures

The angel of the LORD encamps around those who fear Him, and He delivers them. Taste and see that the LORD is good; blessed is the man who takes refuge in Him. Fear the LORD you His saints, for those who fear Him lack nothing (Ps. 34:7-9 NIV).

The LORD is your keeper; The LORD is your shade at your right hand. The sun shall not strike you by day, nor the moon by night. The LORD shall preserve you from all evil; He shall preserve your soul. The LORD shall preserve your going out and your coming in from this time forth, and even forevermore (Ps. 121:5-8 NKJV).

Commit to Memory

1 John 2:15: ***Do not love the world or the things in the world. If anyone loves the world, the love of the Father is not in him.*** **(NKJV)**

The Enemies of God's Children
(Part 3)

Satan – "the great opposer, or adversary, of God and man; the personal name of the devil" *(Nelson's Illustrated Dictionary of the Bible).*

The most infamous of all our enemies is Satan. He is also called the devil, which means slanderer or accuser. He has many titles: the deceiver (Gen. 3:13), the tempter (1 Thess. 3:5), Beelzebub (Matt. 12:24), the wicked one (Matt. 13:19, 38), the ruler of this world (John 12:31), the god of this age (2 Cor. 4:4), Belial (2 Cor. 6:15), the prince of the power of the air (Eph 2:2), and the accuser of our brethren (Rev. 12:10). Each of these titles identifies a particular area of his character. Satan is extremely powerful, but he is still a created being (Ezek. 28:11-19).

He is a fallen angel cast down from heaven as a result of his pride, which led to iniquity. He does not possess creative powers. He is not omnipotent (having unlimited power and authority), and he is not omnipresent (everywhere all the time). His powers are limited to those things described in his titles, which depict his character. When he was cast out of heaven, he retained all of his powers. God never takes back his gifts and callings from anyone (Rom. 11:29).

Satan is effective against many of us because he does not work alone. He and his followers (fallen angels) were present before the creation of mankind. He is well aware of our weaknesses and uses every means available to him to attack those areas of our lives. His primary areas of attack are pride, lust, greed, jealousy, and covetousness.

1. He uses our pride to destroy us (Dan. 4:30-34).
2. He used David's lust to bring sin on his entire house (2 Sam. 11:2, 4, 27)
3. He used the greed of Judas to destroy him (Matt. 26:14-16).
4. He stirred up jealousy in the heart of Saul against David (1 Sam. 18:6-8)
5. He inspired Absalom's covetousness for David's throne, which cost Absalom his life (2 Sam. 15:10-12).

Satan is also the leader of an entire host of fallen angels, comprising an entire kingdom. When Jesus rebuked the Pharisees regarding their wicked thoughts and statement about the power he possessed, He made mention of Satan's kingdom (Matt. 12:22-27).

1. Satan's kingdom began when he was ejected from heaven (Rev. 12:3-9). The stars are believed by many to represent one-third of the angels in heaven, who chose to follow Satan's rebellion and were cast out of heaven along with him.
2. Ultimately all of our battles are against the devil's kingdom (Eph. 6:12).
3. We have all we need to succeed (Isa. 54:17; Luke 10:17-19; 2 Cor. 10:4).

The devil's schemes haven't changed since the beginning. He has always used temptation, deception, and distraction against those who either oppose him or attempt to set themselves free of his control. He is extremely powerful (Dan. 10:7-13); however, his powers are not limitless, and he will always be subjected to God Almighty.

1. He must get permission from God to afflict Christians (Job 2:3-6).
2. If you resist his temptations, he must flee (James 4:7).
3. He cannot contend with the Word of God (Matt. 4:3-10).

As children of God we must not be fearful of the devil. We always are to be mindful of him and his wicked schemes, but we are to fear God and God alone. The devil is by no means to be taken lightly, because he is our enemy. However, if we walk in obedience to God and stay alert, being mindful of his workings, we cannot be affected by his tricks (1 Pet 5:8-9). He can harm us only if he has a part in us. Examine your life daily for anything that is contrary to the character of the Holy Spirit. If you find anything, repent and pray that God will remove it. If you don't, Satan will have access to you and will eventually destroy your life and possibly countless others. If he has no part in you, nothing he does can affect you (John 14:30). Keep these truths in mind.

1. We are to fear God only—with a reverential fear—not Satan (Matt. 10:28)
2. The Holy Spirit is the most powerful force on earth (1 John 4:4)
3. Satan is already defeated (Heb. 2:14)

Meditate on These Scriptures

Those who trust in the LORD are like Mount Zion, which cannot be moved, but abides forever. As the mountains surround Jerusalem, so the LORD surrounds His people from this time forth and forever. For the scepter of wickedness shall not rest on the land allotted to the righteous, lest the righteous reach out their hands to iniquity. Do good, O LORD, to those who are good, and to those who are upright in their hearts. As for such as turn aside to their crooked ways, the LORD shall lead them away with the workers of iniquity. Peace be upon Israel! (Ps. 125 NKJV)

Blessed is everyone who fears the LORD, who walks in His ways. When you eat the labor of your hands, you shall be happy, and it shall be well with you. Your wife shall be like a fruitful vine in the very heart of your house, your children like olive plants all around your table. Behold, thus shall the man be blessed who fears the LORD. The LORD bless you out of Zion, and may you see the good of Jerusalem all the days of your life. Yes, may you see your children's children. Peace be upon Israel! (Ps.128 NKJV)

Commit to Memory

1 John 4:4: ***You, dear children, are from God and have overcome them, because the one who is in you is greater than the one who is in the world.*** **(NIV)**

12

Fear

Fear – "a feeling of reverence, awe, and respect, or an unpleasant emotion caused by a sense of Danger" *(Nelson's Illustrated Dictionary of the Bible).*

Fear – "anxiety caused by real or possible danger, pain, etc.; fright. 2. Awe; reverence" *(Webster's New World Dictionary and Thesaurus).*

As these definitions clearly show, there are two forms of fear—one of God and one from the world. God did not give His children a spirit of fear but of love, power, self-discipline, and adoption (2 Tim. 1:7). However, God is to be feared and awed from a reverential perspective. This type of fear comes from the knowledge of God and leads to wisdom (Prov. 1:7). It is a necessary and healthy fear that humbles the human spirit and enables us to have a proper relationship with our Creator. He is to be awed (Ps. 46:10). Even at the name of our Lord and Savior Jesus Christ, every knee must voluntarily bow (Phil. 2:8-11). Reverence produces the promises of God.

1. The promise of provision to all who fear—reverence Him (Ps. 34:9-10).
2. The promise of healing to all who fear—reverence Him (Mal. 4:2).
3. God's promise of protection to those who fear—reverence Him (Ps. 34:7).

In contrast to a healthy fear of God, the world's fear causes torment, dread, and extreme terror because this present world system belongs to Satan (2 Cor. 4:4; 1 John 5:19). This type of fear is from the adversary, and it will prevent us from serving God in the capacity that He desires of us because we will doubt our own abilities and God's (Judg. 6:11-24). Fear cancels faith because to fear is to disbelieve and disobey God (Matt. 10:28). Fear is one of the most powerful weapons in the devil's arsenal. When the devil manages to get you in a state of fear, he cripples your ministry and prevents you from being effective.

Fear was birthed in the garden after the fall of man. The knowledge of evil brought forth fear, guilt, and shame—fear comes from evil. Mankind's desire to be like God gave the architect of evil, deception, and lies an opportunity to plant the seed of disobedience, which manifested a harvest of sin leading to fear, separation from God, and ultimately death. Unfortunately, many of us never advance in life because of fear. We're too often worried about what others think or what will happen if we fail. That's crippling fear! Notice the beginning of man's fear and its effect on the human race.

1. The beginning of fear (Gen. 3:7-10).
2. The acceptance of fear will destroy your faith (1 Kings 19:1-18).
3. The effect of fear will cancel out all that we have witnessed God do in our lives (Num13: 23-33,14:1-23).4.

The only antidote for fear is faith (Ps. 46:1-7). Faith casts out all fear. Perfect faith is reliance, total obedience, and trust in God—regardless of the circumstances. It means believing that He is exactly whom He says and that He can perform everything that He has promised. Perfect faith builds confidence and comforts the heart.

The power of faith will cancel any fear that we may have. "If we can believe, then we will be relieved." Void of fear, total faith ignites the power of God. These are just a few examples of God's response to total faith.

1. David's faith in God helped him defeat the giant everyone else feared (I Sam. 17:31-51).
2. Shadrach, Meshach, and Abed-Nego were without fear and full of faith (Dan. 3:13-30).
3. Peter's momentary faith produced a miraculous act, but fear cancelled it (Matt. 14:25-31).

The Holy Spirit is our safeguard against fear. He is our proof of adoption into God's Holy family (Rom. 8:14,15). The Spirit is the fulfillment of God's promise and our protection from terror and dread. The Spirit is love, and God is love, and perfect love casts out all fear (1 John 4:15-18). He is also our freedom from any sort of fear caused by demonic attacks from the adversary. Our liberty in the Spirit of God will set us free from torment (2 Cor. 3:17).

Whenever fear attempts to take us captive, we must remind ourselves that it is a spirit that does not belong to us (2 Tim. 1:7). Anything that causes torment is from the adversary and is designed to cancel our faith in God. We can defeat fear by casting down all imaginations and thoughts that give place to fear (2 Cor. 10:3-5). We are to continuously remind ourselves that the Spirit of God lives in us and that He is greater than any wicked force that attempts to destroy our peace (1 John 4:4). Do not fear; just believe God.

Meditate on Theses Scriptures

There is no fear in love; but perfect love casts out fear, because fear involves torment. But he who fears has not been made perfect in love. (1 John 4:18 NKJV)

For you did not receive the spirit of bondage again to fear, but you received the Spirit of adoption by whom we cry out, "Abba, Father." (Rom. 8:15 NKJV)

Commit to Memory

2 Timothy 1:7: ***For God has not given us a spirit of fear, but of power and of love and of a sound mind.*** **(NKJV)**

13

Scriptural Principles For A Successful Life

One of the first major principles of the Bible is that we will reap what we sow (Gen. 1:11, 24-25; 4:1-7; Gal. 6:7). This is the oldest principle in Scripture, and it will not change before the coming of the Lord. As simple as it sounds, many of us just don't seem to be able to grasp this important Bible principle. In order to reap we must sow, regardless of the circumstances. If we want friends, we must show ourselves friendly, if we want affection in our relationships we must be affectionate. If we want success, we must work at what it is we want to be successful in. Can a man withdraw from a bank in which he has not made a deposit? Of course not!

The principle of sowing and reaping applies to everything we do in life. Until we learn to apply this important principle to every single aspect of our lives, we will continue to experience disappointment in our harvests. If the Lord said do unto others what we desire them to do unto us sums up the Law and the Prophets (Matt. 7:7-12), how important must this principle of sowing and reaping be? To do unto others what we desire them to do unto us is the same as sowing and reaping. We should not expect anymore than what we ourselves are willing to give. The Bible speaks frequently of the benefits of sowing.

1. The benefits of sowing to the kingdom of God (Gal. 6:9-10).
2. The dangers of sowing to the flesh versus the benefits of sowing to the Spirit (Gal 6:8).
3. The benefits of generously sowing in your finances (Malachi 3:10-12; 1 Cor. 9:6-8).
4. Sowing peace creates righteousness (James 3:18).

The second principle in Christianity that leads to a successful life is separation from this present world system. First, let me explain what is meant by "the world system." The term refers to the mass media that orchestrates this present world culture and the entire present worldview that points away from God and to man. It is the autonomous mind-set of the masses that says man—not God—rules the world. We must separate ourselves from this world system because the Bible says so. God knows the dangers of His children getting caught up in the world. Here are some examples of what the Bible says about separating from the world.

1. We must separate ourselves from this present world system because it is under the control of the adversary (2 Cor. 4:4; 1 John 5:19).
2. We must learn to use the things of this world but not be dominated by them (1 John 2:15-17).
3. All who seek after this world's goods for their own satisfaction with no real regard for God displease Him (Rev. 3:15-19).
4. We are not citizens of this present world (Phil. 3:20).

5. This present world system will never accept a child of God (John 15:18-20; 17:13-23).

We should remember that separating from the world does not mean isolating ourselves from everyone or everything in the world (that would be impossible). It simply means holding the principles of Scripture in a much higher regard than the things of this world. This means our daily walk should reveal humility, faith, confidence, and love for God, others, and ourselves alike. We should not follow every trend the world designs just to fit in. Rather than follow the world, every Christian should be a positive example for the world to see–we are the light of the world (Matt. 5:13-16)!

The final scriptural principle that will lead us to a successful life is walking in the Spirit on a daily basis. This simply means having your mind focused on the things of God on a daily basis and living a life of total obedience. Walking in the Spirit is sometimes referred to as walking in righteousness. Walking simply means living.

1. We can't walk in the Spirit if we allow the things of this present world—TV, gossip, clubs, or any material thing that we put before God—to dominate us (Rom. 6:16).
2. It is impossible to serve God and still hold on to the things of the world (Matt. 6:24).
3. If we are walking in the Spirit, we will be mindful of those with whom we associate. If our friends/associates don't accept Jesus Christ as their Savior, they shouldn't be our friends/associates. There are no exceptions to this rule (1 Cor. 15:33; 2 Cor. 6:14-18).
4. We must read and study the Bible daily to be approved by God (2 Tim. 2:15).

5. Finally, we must be doers of the Word (James 1:21-27).

Many of us are not successful because we really do not live for God. Not one of us is will ever be perfect; however; if we know the truth, we will be held accountable (James 4:17). We must make a decision to live a life of obedience to God or to the world system. To have a successful life, we must follow God's commands. Success in the world does not necessarily equate to a successful life. Seek success God's way!

Meditate on These Scriptures

"No one can serve two masters. Either he will hate the one and love the other, or he will be devoted to the one and despise the other. You cannot serve both God and money." (Matt. 6:24 NIV)

Delight yourself also in the LORD, and He shall give you the desires of your heart. Commit your way to the LORD, trust also in Him, and He shall bring it to pass. (Ps. 37:4-5 NKJV)

Commit to Memory

Isaiah 1:19-20: ***"If you are willing and obedient, you shall eat the good of the land; but if you refuse and rebel, you shall be devoured by the sword"; for the mouth of the LORD has spoken.*** **(NKJV)**

14

Prayer
(Part 1)

What is the purpose of prayer, and why is it important to us? Prayer is the believer's direct communication line to God. There are a number of reasons why prayer is important for Christians. As previously stated, prayer gives us direct access to God and enables us to enter into the presence of God and offer our praise, thanksgiving, repentance, and requests. Praying is also an act of obedience to the Word of God. Throughout the entire Bible, the children of God are told to pray for themselves and others—even our enemies. Throughout the Bible we can find examples of men and women of God who performed miraculous deeds through faith-filled prayers.

Jesus Christ modeled the perfect example of a prayerful life. He prayed to the Father daily. He often would arise early or go off on His own to be alone with the Father, and we should do likewise. When He warned His disciples to watch and pray (Matt. 26:41), Jesus brought to light a very important fact about prayer: our prayers strengthen the Spirit living in us and give Him dominion over our flesh. Without a dedicated prayer life, our flesh will fail us time after time. However, our lives must be clean to enter into the presence of God (Ps. 24:3-4). If we participate in sinful behavior and do not repent, God will not hear our prayers (Ps. 66:18).

However, if we repent and confess our sins, God will forgive us (1 John 1:9). Repentance is necessary if we desire to communicate with Almighty God. Because He is holy, we must enter His awesome presence in holiness. Below is a list of important principles regarding prayer that we should always take into account before we pray.

1. The crucifixion of our Savior Jesus Christ made it possible for us to enter the presence of the Almighty God (Mark 15:37-38; cf. Exod. 26:31-37) because it permanently removed the separation between God and man.
2. Because we are in the presence of God when we pray, we must come in total humility and reverence as standing before His throne (Phil. 2:10-11; Rev. 4:4-11).
3. If we are living in obedience to the Word of God, we can be confident and expectant that He will answer our prayers (1 Pet. 3:12; 1 John 3:21-24).
4. When our prayers are combined with faith, it will remove all anxiety and give us comfort and total peace through Jesus Christ (Phil. 4:6-7).
5. Faith-filled prayer is extremely powerful (Matt. 21:22; James 5:13-18).
6. We must learn to pray for those things that are in His will for us (1 John 5:14,15).

Prayer is the most important aspect of the Christian's life because this is the only way we can communicate with God. He communicates to us through His Word, people, and circumstances, but we must communicate with Him through prayer. Careful study of the Bible will reveal to us that every servant of God, including Jesus, spent much of his or her time in prayer, seeking God for help, comfort, provision, and protection and offering Him thanksgiving and praise. Here are some good examples of how prayer impacted the lives of those who served God.

1. Daniel made it his custom to pray three times a day (Dan. 6:10). Others also recognized him as a praying man and a servant of God (Dan. 6:16, 19-20).
2. The apostle Paul, the author of thirteen books in the New Testament, always expressed the importance of prayer (1 Thess. 5:17-18; 1 Tim. 2:1-5, 8).
3. Our Savior Jesus Christ modeled a life of prayer, praying to the Father daily for Himself and others (Matt 14:22-23; 26:36-39). When Jesus knew it was time for Him to depart, He prayed to the Father for His disciples (John 17:9-26).
4. Hannah poured her heart out before the throne of God, praying with diligence that her request would be honored, and God answered her prayer (1 Sam. 1:1-20; 2:1-10).
5. Elijah was a man like many of us yet his prayer shut up the heavens so that it did not rain for three years (James 5:17,18).

Prayer is an extremely valuable resource for all Christians. It can provide protection from the weakness of our flesh (Matt. 26:41), it can be like miraculous medicine for the sick (James 5:14), and when we pray in total faith, it is the key to God's promises (Matt. 21:22). However, we must pray for those things that are in His will for our lives (1 John 5:14-15), and we must always keep in mind the importance of using the power of prayer to intercede on behalf of others (Eph. 6:18). Prayer should come directly from our hearts. There is no need for us to practice prayer or attempt to remember any particular lines.

Prayer is personal communication with God, and it does not require that we use big words or deep terminology. God knows our hearts and desires. We just need to come before His presence with a clear heart and be who we are. He already knows exactly what we are in need of and what our desires are (Matt. 6:5-15; Luke 12:22-34). Because God knew that we sometimes would struggle in our prayer life, He provided help for us (Rom. 8:26-30, 34). Just as we desire to hear from our own children and be an integral part of their lives, so God desires to hear from us. If you don't have a regular prayer life, start now. God is waiting to hear from you.

Take notice of these three important facts about prayer as you begin your personal communication line with God.

1. If we're righteous, God will answer our prayers (James 5:15-18).
2. We should always pray to the Father in the name of His Son Jesus Christ. Why? Because the Bible says so (John 14:12-14; 15:15-17; 16:23-28).
3. Finally, we are to always pray and not grow weary when our prayers and requests are not answered immediately (Luke 18:1-8). God is not obligated to answer our prayers according to our desired time schedule. His time is not like ours (2 Pet. 3:8-9).

Meditate on These Scriptures

"Father, I desire that they also whom You gave Me may be with Me where I am, that they may behold my glory which you have given Me; for You loved Me before the foundation of the world. O righteous Father! The world has not known You, but I have known You; and these have known that You sent

Me. And I have declared to them Your name, and will declare it, that the love with which You loved Me may be in them, and I in them." (John 17:24-26 NKJV)

But at midnight Paul and Silas were praying and singing hymns to God, and the prisoners were listening to them. Suddenly there was a great earthquake, so that the foundations of the prison were shaken; and immediately all the doors were open and everyone's chains were loosed. And the keeper of the prison, awaking from sleep and seeing the prison doors open, supposing the prisoners had fled, drew his sword and was about to kill himself. But Paul called with a loud voice, saying, "Do yourself no harm, for we are all here."

Then he called for a light, ran in, and fell down trembling before Paul and Silas. And he brought them out and said, "Sirs, what must I do to be saved?" So they said, Believe on the Lord Jesus Christ, and you will be saved, you and your household." Then they spoke the Word of the Lord to him and to all who were in his house. And he took them the same hour of the night and washed their stripes. And immediately he and all his family were baptized.

Now when he had brought them into his house, he set food before them; and he rejoiced, having believed in God with all his household. (Acts 16:25-34 NKJV)

Commit to Memory

Mathew 26:41: ***"Watch and pray, lest you enter into temptation. The spirit indeed is willing, but the flesh is weak."*** **(NKJV)**

Principles of Prayer
(Part 2)

Maintaining a clean heart is the first and main principle of prayer. It is essential if we want our prayers to be heard. Because we serve a holy God who cannot disregard sin, we must examine our hearts daily for any sign of iniquity (sin); and if we identify any, we must pray the prayer of repentance. We must ask the LORD to cleanse our hearts and minds on a daily basis. This is the key to opening our communication line to God. We must always remember that sin will short-circuit the power of our prayers (Ps. 66:18; Mark 11:25-26). Jesus told His disciples and the multitudes of people to first reconcile any differences they had with another before they made their offering at the LORD'S altar (Matt. 5:21-24).

The next step we must take to develop a powerful prayer life is to establish a personal relationship with God—sometimes described as an intimate relationship with God. This is essential if we desire to have powerful prayers. This close and personal relationship with God will increase our trust in Him by revealing to us His sovereignty. This close relationship with God is established through fellowship with Him. To fellowship with God means to spend time with Him by reading and meditating on His Word. The more time we pend reading and meditating on His Word, the better we will know Him.

The better we know Him, the easier it will be to pray. Once we learn of His kind, merciful, and loving character, we will never be able to get enough of Him. The psalmist said, "O taste and see that the LORD is good" (Ps. 34:8a). This is a perfect picture of one who truly had personal experiences with God. This relationship with God will develop our faith as we witness His awesome power working in our lives. Complete faith in God is the only way our prayers will be answered (Matt. 21:22). Anything less than this kind of faith in God is sin (Heb. 11:6). We will also learn God's will for His people through daily study of the Bible.

This is why studying the Word of God is so important to our prayer life–it teaches us what to pray for. To have effective prayers, we must know His will for our lives. It is simply impossible to know God's will without reading, meditating on, and studying the Bible on a daily basis. Once we begin this practice, His will for our lives will be plain to see. We will also notice that our prayer requests will begin to change from focusing on ourselves to focusing on others. Once we really know and understand God's will for His people, our prayers will be far more effective (1 John 5:14-15).

The next principle may seem simple, but most of us don't get it. Our prayers must be specific! If someone were to ask you what it was that you really needed or wanted, could you answer? When we come before God's presence in prayer, we must know what we desire of Him(even though He already knows), and we must be clear about it. If we have followed the first two steps (maintaining a clean heart and developing an intimate relationship with God), this one will come through the guidance of the Holy Spirit. At this point our prayers should not resemble a kid's Christmas list. Remember, God is not our personal catalog or supplier.

God did not create us for the sole purpose of taking our personal orders and granting our every single desire. However, He will supply all of our needs (Ps. 37:25-26; Phil. 4:19), and He will bless us with our hearts' desires when they are in accord with His will for us (Ps. 37:4-5; 1 John 5:14-15), if we are living in obedience to Him. However, we must be specific! Jesus asked blind Bartimaeus what was it that he desired of Him when surely He already knew that Bartimaeus desired to receive his sight (Mark 10:46-52)

To simply pray to God, asking Him to bless us, isn't specific enough. Consider that every morning that God awakes us in our right minds with the use of all our limbs and faculties means He has blessed us, because we have another opportunity to spread the gospel and earn treasures in heaven. God already knows what's on our minds and in our hearts, but He wants us to be specific. Notice what Jesus said to Bartimaeus: "What do you want Me to do for you?" (Mark 10:46-52). Certainly Jesus, being the visible representation of the invisible God, knew what blind Bartimaeus wanted Him to do.

The only reason He would have asked him that question was because He wanted Bartimaeus to be specific about his need and to express his faith that he believed the Lord could do what he desired of Him. Take notice of these three important points that should be highly considered as we develop in our prayer life.

1. Seek God in faith and confidence without any doubt (James 1:5-8).
2. Make your request clear to God (Phil. 4:6-7).
3. The specific prayers of the saints are powerful (James 5:13-18).

As we walk in the spirit of meekness and humility, our prayers also should represent the selfsame spirit. This means we should not lust after the things of the world to identify ourselves with those of the world. The focus of our prayers should be on those whom we know are lost and suffering. We should begin to pray more for those whom God has placed in positions of leadership (even outside the church). As we begin to mature spiritually, God will place a greater burden on our hearts for souls. At this point our prayers will be very effective. Here are four points that will guide us in our prayer life.

1. If we allow our fleshly desires to control us, they will eventually dominate our prayer life and our relationship with God (James 4:1-6). This will not happen if the Spirit of God leads us.
2. A strong desire for worldly things is in opposition to God's will (1 John 2:15-17).
3. Our humility is revealed in the way that we pray (Matt. 6:5-8).
4. The Lord gave us a model of how we ought to pray (Matt. 6:9-13).

Finally, we must be persistent in prayer. If our prayers aren't answered, we must not faint but be persistent in prayer, believing God for all His promises. Jesus told His disciples a powerful parable about persistence that is extremely relevant to us (Luke 18:1-8). Our steadfast persistence shows our faith in God—if we believe God, we'll keep on praying. Take notice of these six points that can help us as we grow in our prayer life.

1. Ask and keep asking (Luke 11:9-13; Matt. 7:7-8 Amplified Bible).
2. God is not a respecter of persons and will answer your prayers (James 5:16-18).
3. Our prayers are stored up in heaven (Rev. 8:3-4).

4. Rejoice and always pray with thanksgiving (1 Thess. 5:16-18).
5. The LORD is not slow; He's patient (2 Pet. 3:9).
6. We are always to pray to the Father in the name of His Son (Matt. 6:5-13).

If you haven't been praying on a daily basis, start now. Use these principles to help you as develop a powerful prayer life and a wonderful relationship with God.

Meditate on These Scriptures

> ***Therefore I also, after I heard of your faith in the Lord Jesus and your love for all the saints, do not cease to give thanks for you, making mention of you in my prayers: that the GOD of our Lord Jesus Christ, the Father of glory, may give to you the spirit of wisdom and revelation in the knowledge of Him, the eyes of your understanding being enlightened; that you may know what is the hope of His calling, what are the riches of the glory of His inheritance in the saints, and what is the exceeding greatness of His power toward us who believe, according to the working of*** His mighty power which He worked in Christ when He raised Him from the dead and seated Him at His right hand in heavenly places, far above all principality and power and might and dominion, and every name that is named, not only in this age but also in that which is to come. And He put all things under His feet and gave Him to be head over all things to the church, which is His body, the fullness of Him who fills all in all (Eph. 1:15-23 NKJV).

> For this reason we also, since the day we heard it, do not cease to pray for you, and to ask that you may be

filled with the knowledge of His will in all wisdom and spiritual understanding; that you may walk worthy of the Lord, fully pleasing Him, being fruitful in every good work and increasing in the knowledge of God; strengthened with all might, according to His glorious power, for all patience and longsuffering with joy; giving thanks to the Father who has qualified us to be partakers of the inheritance of the saints in light (Col. 1:9-12 NKJV).

Commit to Memory

Hebrews 11:6: ***But without faith it is impossible to please Him, for he who comes to God must believe that He is, and that He is a rewarder of those who diligently seek Him.*** **(NKJV)**

Preparing Our Hearts for Prayer (Part 3)

Before we enter into God's presence through prayer, we must fully examine ourselves. If we know that we have said or done something that was offensive to God, we must first confess it and repent of it in our prayers (1 John 1:9; Matt. 12:36-37). Only then are we ready to enter into the presence of God. We must enter into the presence of almighty God with reverence and total humility. I have intentionally mentioned humility and faith over and over because of their importance. We must understand that God is holy. When we approach His throne, we must have clean hearts and minds. That means letting go of all animosity (Mark 11:25-26).

Often our prayers are not answered because we are not properly prepared before we attempt to enter the presence of God. He is the sinless Creator of the universe. He cannot look upon sin and He cannot hear our prayers if we are living in sin (Ps. 66:18). Consider the fact that God the Father turned His back on God the Son (Jesus Christ) when Christ took on all of our sins (Matt. 27:45-50). How then can He hear us if we habitually sin? We must continually walk in holiness. Take notice of these examples in Scripture that show how Lord's awesome presence demands our total reverence.

1. God's awesome presence demands reverence and fear (Exod. 3:1-6; John 18:1-5; Acts 9:1-7).
2. No one can stand in the presence of the Savior and Creator (Rev. 1:10-18).
3. Every living thing must bow to the Lord (Phil. 2: 8-11; Rev. 4:8-11; 7:9-12).

When we pray we must believe that God can and will do what He promised (Mark 11:20-24). Harboring disbelief is a sin and will definitely cause our prayers to go unanswered. Because faith is the primary aspect in serving God, the lack thereof is unpleasing to Him (Heb. 11:4-6). Faith and obedience go hand in hand. One cannot have faith and walk in disobedience. If you believe and love God, you will do what the Bible says (John 14:19-24). Our love for the LORD will be exemplified in our prayers. If we truly love God, we will pray often and with total faith. Here are three things we should consider as we pray.

1. God promised to answer prayers of faith (Matt 21:18-22).
2. We should never question, just believe (James 1:5-7).
3. Nothing is impossible with God (Luke 1:26-37).

We must always be mindful that Jesus Christ is the authority and the power, and in His name we are to pray. Jesus Christ is the mediator between God and man and sits at the right hand of the Father, interceding on behalf of all the saints (Acts 2:32,33; Rom. 8:34; 1 Tim. 2:5,6). The fact that Jesus Christ intercedes on our behalf and the Holy Spirit helps us as we pray (Rom. 8:26,27) should build our confidence toward God. We have not earned anything, but because of the sacrifice of our Lord and God's grace we can feel confident approaching the throne of God through prayer.

This is the substance that builds our faith. The Bible is clear about the Lord's authority.

1. Jesus Christ received all the authority from the Father (Matt. 28:18-20).
2. Only through Jesus Christ can we get to the Father (John 14:6-7).
3. The Lord promised to answer the prayers of all believers who ask in His Holy name (John 14:12-14).

Prayer is vital to all Christians, and it should be at the forefront of all of our lives. However, we must remember that the adversary will do all he can to prevent us from establishing a powerful prayer life. The devil knows the power of prayer and will attempt to discourage us by telling us that it's OK for us to continue in a weak, inconsistent prayer life. He will do whatever he can to hinder our prayers (Dan. 10:12-13). How many times have you noticed that just before you begin to pray or read the Bible, you either get sleepy or forget who or what you intended to pray for or about?

I believe this is a scheme from the devil designed to prevent us from interceding on behalf of those who are blinded (2 Cor. 4:4) and to prevent us from developing and growing spiritually. However, the God we serve is able to keep us from falling as long as we're walking in obedience. Let's begin to prepare our hearts for prayer by using these biblical principles and allow the Spirit of the Lord to empower our prayers. We must begin to take advantage of this wonderful grace that God has granted to us through Jesus Christ our Lord, who is a true High Priest interceding on our behalf (Heb. 7:23-27).

Meditate on These Scriptures

Likewise the Spirit also helps in our weakness. For we do not know what we should pray for as we ought, but the Spirit Himself makes intercession for us with groanings which cannot be uttered. Now He who searches the hearts knows what the mind of the Spirit is, because He makes intercession for the saints according to the will of God. (Rom. 8:26-27 NKJV)

Therefore I exhort first of all that supplications, prayers, intercessions, and giving of thanks be made for all men, for kings and all who are in authority, that we may lead a quiet and peaceable life in all godliness and reverence. For this is good and acceptable in the sight of God our Savior, who desires all men to be saved and to come to the knowledge of the truth. For there is one God and one mediator between God and men, the Man Christ Jesus, who gave Himself a ransom for all, to be testified in due time, for which I was appointed a preacher and an apostle—I am speaking the truth in Christ and not lying—a teacher of the Gentiles in faith and truth.

I desire therefore that the men pray everywhere, lifting up holy hands, without wrath and doubting (1 Tim. 2:1-8 NKJV).

Commit to Memory

Matthew 21:22: ***"And whatever things you ask in prayer, believing, you will receive."*** **(NKJV)**

15

Self-Examination

We must take the time to examine ourselves on a daily basis if we desire to fully develop spiritually. Self-examination is the best way to measure spiritual growth and to uncover strongholds and yokes that exist in our lives. Our natural instinct is to recognize sin in the lives of others, while harboring some of the same things in our own lives. There is nothing wrong with judging those who claim to be children of God (1 Cor. 5:11-13), but we must first examine ourselves. This is not something that comes naturally, but if we practice examining ourselves on a daily basis it will become second nature.

The best way to start this process is by using examples and principles from the Bible to guide and instruct us on what God desires of us and then begin to apply what we learn to our lives. We must learn to measure ourselves by God's standards and not by what others are doing. Often we may look at the lives of others and use that as a barometer to measure our own character. We may think that if someone we know who claims to be a Christian is doing far worse than we are, then we're OK. That type of thinking is not from God; it's from Satan. If we know better, God will judge us accordingly (Luke 12:41-48; James 4:13-17).

Here is a list of four very important points regarding self-examination. Taking these points into consideration will help us to understand the importance of examining our lives on a daily basis and the danger of disregarding this important scriptural principle.

1. Our first judgment must be upon ourselves (Matt. 7:1-5).
2. The lack of self-examination causes us to sin against God (1 Cor. 11:27-32).
3. Self-examination will lead us to a life of reality, truth, and clear direction (Gal. 6:3-5).
4. Self-examination will reveal whether or not we are walking in holiness (2 Cor. 13:5).

As we question why there isn't any spiritual power in our lives or in the church, we must evaluate our personal relationship with God. Daily examination of ourselves will reveal to us what is missing in our personal relationship with God—or whether we have one at all. This is vital if we want to walk in confidence toward God. The process of examining ourselves will reveal to us what steps we need to take to improve our relationship with God, which will definitely enable us to walk in power (confidence toward God).

Part of the process of examining self involves evaluating our character according to Scripture. But how do we do this? Examine your character by answering these questions. Do you render evil for evil? Have you forgiven those who have hurt you in your past? Do you hold grudges for long periods of time? Do you gossip? Are you a fornicator? Are you a habitual liar? Do you seek a church office while your own household is in a mess? Do you confess Jesus Christ openly? Do you pray for leaders in the church and the world? After you've answered these questions from your own personal standpoint (or opinion), take a look at the topics below and consider what the Bible says about some of these same questions.

1. It is not our job to return the favor to the wicked (Rom. 12:19-21).
2. You can be forgiven only if you are willing to forgive (Matt. 6:14-15; Eph. 4:26-27).
3. Do you practice true religion (James 1:21-27)?
4. Avoid corrupt communication (Eph. 4:29-32).
5. Your body belongs to God (1 Cor. 6:9-11, 18-20).
6. Liars are of the devil (John 8:44).
7. Leaders must first learn to lead at home (1 Tim 3:1-13).
8. Do you confess Jesus openly (Matt. 10:32-33)?
9. Does your life model a true love for the Lord (John 14:21-24)?
10. Are you mature enough to love those who don't necessarily love you (Matt. 5:43-48)?
11. Do you pray for everyone (1 Tim. 2:1-4)?

Pray daily that God will reveal to you any habitual sin that may still exist in your life. Ask God to strengthen you in the areas of your life in which you feel weak and to remove any yoke that may be preventing you from growing spiritually. The Bible says to let your requests be made known unto God (Phil. 4:6). This means we should be plain and specific regarding our petitions to God. Ask yourself these very important questions and answer them honestly. Your honest answers to these questions can help you to evaluate any changes you may need to make in your Christian walk. Do you spend any time in prayer or studying the Bible? Do you spend most of your time on the phone, watching TV, or just walking around in the mall? How much time do you spend surfing the Internet? Where is your treasure (Matt. 6:21)? Are your motives fueled primarily by personal gain? We will never reach perfection as long as we occupy these fleshly bodies, however, God desires that we walk in obedience not perfection. We must begin to examine ourselves on a daily basis and make changes when necessary. We need to pray to God in the name of Jesus Christ for His grace to enable us to make the necessary changes in our lives to please Him.

Meditate on These Scriptures

> Lean on, trust in, and be confident in the Lord with all your heart and mind and do not rely on your own insight or understanding. In all your ways know, recognize, and acknowledge him, and He will direct and make straight and plain your paths. (Prov. 3:5-6 Amplified Bible)

> Everyone who sins breaks the law; in fact, sin is lawlessness. But you know that He appeared so that He might take away our sins. And in Him is no sin. No one who lives in Him keeps on sinning. No one who continues to sin has either seen Him or known Him. Dear children, do not let anyone lead you astray. He who does what is right is righteous, just as He is righteous. He who does what is sinful is from the devil, because the devil has been sinning from the beginning. The reason the Son of God appeared was to destroy the devil's work.
>
> No one who is born of God will continue to sin, because God's seed remains in Him; he cannot go on sinning, because he has been born of God. This is how we know who the children of God are and who the children of the devil are: Anyone who does not

do what is right is not a child of God; nor is anyone who does not love his brother, (1 John 3:4-10 NIV)

Commit to Memory

Lamentations 3:40: ***Let us search out and examine our ways, and turn back to the LORD.*** **(NKJV)**

16

Obedience
(Part 1)

Total obedience to the Word of God is paramount in the life of all Christians. The key to walking in the fullness of God's blessings and grace is obedience to His commands. There is no substitute for obedience, and anything else is sin. Praying, fasting, tithing, giving to the poor, and any other form of personal sacrifice is worthless if we are disobedient to the commands of God. Our obedience to God is a sign of our faith in Him and our love for Him. We don't need to be theologians to understand that if we love and believe God we will be obedient to what the Bible instructs us to do. Our obedience leads to protection, provision, and promotion.

1. Promise of protection (Deut. 28:7).
2. Promise of provision and freedom from debt (Deut. 28:12).
3. Promise of leadership (Deut 28:13).

Why aren't these promises being fulfilled in the lives of so many of us? We may all have our personal opinions regarding why some of God's promises are not being fulfilled in our lives or the lives of others. However, to base anything related to God on our opinions, without using the Bible as our barometer, is to lean on our own understanding and therefore guarantee that our analysis will be flawed. This is also disobedience. The Bible says in all thy ways to acknowledge Him (Prov. 3:5-6). We are to always use Scripture and not our personal opinions to interpret the things of God. These truths will be helpful.

1. Iniquity (sin) shuts off our communication line with God (Ps. 66:18).
2. We will always have to pay the consequences of our actions (Gal. 6:7).
3. Even little, "white" lies or so-called small sins can destroy our lives (1 Cor. 5:6).

Faith and obedience are no strangers to each other. It is impossible to be obedient to the Word of God without faith. Our obedience to God is the substance of our faith in Him. Simply put, if we believe Him, we'll obey Him. However, as simple as it seems to just obey the Word of God, most of us struggle as a result of our disobedience. If we claim to have faith yet walk in disobedience, we deceive ourselves. You can't have one without the other! Look at these examples of faith below and the powerful statement that the Lord makes regarding obedience to His Word. These are our examples.

1. To have faith means to trust, believe, obey, and rely totally upon God (Heb.11:17-22).
2. If you love the Lord, you will be obedient to His Word (John 14:23-24).

How do we know if we are being obedient to God? If we want to find out if we are being obedient to God, we only have to ask ourselves whether we are doing what the Bible says. This is not a question of whether or not you follow any type of ceremonial laws—we are under grace and not the law; therefore the law does not bind us. However, this is not an open door to autonomy. The Bible was inspired by God to instruct us and protect us.

The holy Creator of the universe knows what's best for those whom He created. That's why it's so important for us to walk in obedience to His Word. With so many examples in the Bible of those who failed as a result of disobedience and those who prospered as a result of obedience to God, why wouldn't we want be obedient to God more than anything else in the world? It is beneficial to be obedient to the Word of God for the present and the future. The Bible says, "The earth is the LORD'S and everything in it" (Ps. 24:1). Obedience prepares us to receive from the LORD. However, our obedience should not be motivated by personal gain from God. We obey Him, because He first loved us.

We obey Him because He gave His only begotten Son as a sacrificial payment for us. We obey Him because He delivered us from eternal damnation. We obey Him because He put on flesh and humbled Himself, becoming like the created being so that He could pay our debt. We obey Him because He's GOD! Obedience can be a challenge because it's not always the popular thing to do. Take King Saul for instance. He obeyed the voice of the people because it was pleasing to the people, and he lost his kingdom to David (1 Sam. 13:1-15). Disobedience can be costly and even deadly.

Take a look at the list below, and answer the five questions regarding obedience to the Bible. After you've answered the questions, compare your answers to the Word of God. These types of exercises can help us identify those areas of our lives that we need to address. Once we have identified those areas of disobedience in our lives, we can take the proper steps toward making changes (prayer, submission, and simply doing what the Bible says).

1. "You shall have no other gods before Me" (Exod. 20:3, the first commandment). Do you put anything before God (Matt 6:24; Rom. 6:16)?
2. Do you study the Word of God (2 Tim. 2:15)?
3. Do you humble yourself and give reverence to the LORD (Phil. 2:10-11)?
4. Do you pray daily (Matt. 26:41; Phil. 4:6-7; 1 Thess. 5:16-18)?
5. Are you in the service of making disciples (Matt. 28:18-20)?

We must always be mindful that pride and selfishness are the two main characteristics of our adversary, Satan (Isa. 14:10-15). If we continuously display his characteristics in our lives, then we are led by him and not by God. The Christian life means giving freely of our time and resources and not always expecting something in return. Even the LORD GOD says that you must give in order that you may receive (Mal. 3:10). The principle of sowing and reaping will always remain. Sowing obedience to God's Word will reap a harvest of eternal life in His awesome presence.

The Lord described the wise individual as the one who obeys His Word (Matt. 7:24), which would imply that walking in obedience to God's Word builds wisdom. Along with the wisdom that we acquire through obedience to the Word of God comes knowledge and understanding (Prov. 2:6). We need God's wisdom, which springs from obedience, in order to effectively use the knowledge we acquire from His instruction. A life of obedience to God is a life of promise and purpose. Make every attempt to walk in obedience to the Word of God, and watch how He responds favorably to you.

Meditate on These Scriptures

We are confident, yes, well pleased rather to be absent from the body and to be present with the Lord. Therefore we make it our aim, whether present or absent, to be well pleasing to Him. For we must all appear before the judgment seat of Christ, that each one may receive the things done in the body, according to what he has done, whether good or bad. Knowing, therefore, the terror of the Lord, we persuade men; but we are well known to God, and I also trust are well known in your conscience. (2 Cor. 5:8-11 NKJV)

Now when they came to Marah, they could not drink the waters of Marah, for they were bitter. Therefore the name of it was called Marah. And the people complained against Moses, saying, "What shall we drink? So he cried out to the LORD, and the LORD showed him a tree. When he cast it into the waters, the waters were made sweet. There He made a statute and an ordinance for them, and there He tested them, and said, "If you diligently heed the voice of the LORD your God and do what is right in His sight, give ear to His commandments and keep all His statutes, I will put none of the diseases on you which I have brought on the Egyptians. For I am the LORD who heals you." (Exod. 15:23-26 NKJV)

Commit to Memory

Psalm 119:9: ***How can a young man cleanse his way? By taking heed according to your word.*** **(NKJV)**

Obedience and the Desired Character
(Part 2)

Obedience to authority must be observed as unto God because He appoints all leaders and governments. The church is to set the example of such obedience to authority. Jesus said, "You are the light of the world. A city that is set on a hill cannot be hidden" (Matt 5:14 NKJV). We must be the living example for those in who are in darkness (Matt. 5:15). The Christian example of obedience starts at home with our parents/guardians and extends to local governments and all who are in leadership. God establishes all authority (Rom. 13:1-8); even the leaders and governments that we are not pleased with could not exist if God did not allow them to exist (Dan. 2:21).

Ultimately, the sovereign LORD is in control of all governments and officials. Even those establishments that are wicked and ruled by the adversary could not stand if God chose to tear them down. God's omnipotence protects those who belong to Him from being harmed by wicked leaders and establishments (Ps. 34:7). Often we ask why God allows these establishments to operate if they are so wicked? This is a perfect example of grace and free will. He allows people their own choice to follow what they choose—whether sin leading to death or obedience and righteousness leading to eternal life.

As I have previously stated in this book, our obedience to God is our way of showing that we believe Him and love Him because He has done so much for us. So because of our love for the LORD, we obey; and in our acts of obedience to authorities, we're actually obeying God. Our obedience becomes like instruction to our children, friends, coworkers, and others. This is how we allow our light to shine for everyone to see. People take notice of our obedience to the law and authorities, and then we have an opportunity to testify without speaking—our actions and conduct do all the speaking for us (1 Pet. 3:13-16). Good behavior gives opportunity for witnessing.

We also must learn to be obedient in submission to others. Many Christian marriages struggle because wives refuse to submit to their husbands in obedience to the Bible (1 Pet. 3:1-2). In many cases this is a result of a husband who doesn't render to his wife her just due. However, two wrongs will never equal a right, and we are not to render evil for evil. A very important point that many wives don't understand fully is that submission to their husband is not actually to him but to God. Through a wife's submission to her husband, the Spirit can lead him to Christ by her humble and submissive testimony.

Submission at our workplace and in the church is important for career advancement and church effectiveness. Submitting to your boss/supervisor as opposed to constantly challenging his/her authority can lead to career advancement. It is difficult to receive consideration for promotion if you're considered someone who defies authority and can't get along with management. In the church we must learn to submit to the leaders God has appointed. In too many cases the church of God is divided as a result of prideful individuals who refuse to submit to the direction of the church leadership.

We must be mindful that God is always in control. If it is not of God, He can dismantle it; and if it is of God, He will be glorified.

If we don't feel that we can submit to the leadership at our church, we should leave. It is far better to leave than to sin against God. We must then examine ourselves for a spirit of pride. If it is pride that will not allow us to submit to the leadership of the church, we must repent and ask God through His Holy Spirit to help us vanquish pride from every area of our lives. Once we have been delivered from the spirit of pride, we will be able to submit willingly and freely to every form of leadership, whether it is in church or on our jobs. Here are three aspects of submission that are very important.

1. Mutual submission is required in marriage (Eph. 5:21-33).
2. We are to submit to the shepherd that God appoints (Heb. 13:17).
3. Submission to God enables us to resist the devil (James 4:7).

The Christian life should exemplify a life of humility and selflessness. We should be quick to esteem others above ourselves because of our relationship with God and what we know that He has prepared for us. This should be easy. This is what builds our confidence—not in ourselves but in Him. We know that He will cause all things to work out for our good, and if He is for us, who can be against us (Rom. 8:28, 31)? Because of these truths, we can be pleased to humble ourselves and exalt others, because at the appointed time we know that He will exalt us.

1. We are to submit, humble ourselves, and willingly elevate others (Phil. 2:3-4).
2. Seek to fellowship with those who walk in humility and love (Rom. 12:16).
3. God exalts the humble (1 Pet. 5:5-7).

Forgiveness is essentially the key to our salvation. God sent His Son to die on a cross so that we could be forgiven for our trespasses. Because we were forgiven, we must forgive others. Obedience means following the example of Jesus Christ. If the Lord were not forgiving, we would be without hope. But thanks be to God for His love and grace, which led Him to make the ultimate sacrifice for mankind (Rom. 5:6-8). Now, how could we be disobedient and hard-hearted, refusing to forgive those who have offended us? As we have freely received His grace, we must also freely extend grace to others. Take notice of what the Bible says about forgiveness.

1. We must be willing to forgive, without keeping count of offenses (Matt. 18:21-22).
2. Forgiveness is a key to answered prayers (Mark 11:23-26; Ps. 66:18; Eph. 4:26-27).
3. If we want to receive God's grace, we must be forgiving (Matt. 6:14-15).

The character of all Christians should resemble that of our Savior Jesus Christ. He, being the visible representation of the invisible God, exemplified pure humility and obedience by taking on flesh and becoming a human being to pay our sin debt in full. In the history of mankind there has never been another such a sacrifice—nor will there ever be. Our Savior Jesus Christ, though being equal with God, humbled Himself and was obedient all the way to the cross (John 1:1-5, 14:5-11; Col. 1:15-18; 1 John 5:7). Let this be our example of humility and obedience. Here are three important points that exemplify the character of a Christian.

1. We must strive to have the mind of our Lord (Phil. 2:5-8).
2. If we pray and study daily, we will have the mind of Christ (1 Cor. 2:16) and we will be walking in the Spirit in the victorious Christian life (Gal. 5:16).
3. Most importantly our character should display the fruit of the Holy Spirit (Gal. 5:22-23).

Meditate on These Scriptures

Let every soul be subject to the governing authorities. For there is no authority except from God, and the authorities that exist are appointed by God. Therefore whoever resists the authority resists the ordinance of God, and those who resist will bring judgment on themselves. For rulers are not a terror to good works, but to evil. Do you want to be unafraid of the authority? Do what is good, and you will have praise from the same. For he is God's minister to you for good. But if you do evil, be afraid; for he does not bear the sword in vain; for he is God's minister, an avenger to execute wrath on him who practices evil. Therefore you must be subject, not only because of wrath but also for conscience' sake. (Rom. 13:1-5 NKJV)

Of His own will He brought us forth by the word of truth, that we might be a kind of first fruits of His creatures. So then, my beloved brethren, let every man be swift to hear, slow to speak, slow to wrath; for wrath does not produce the righteousness of God. Therefore lay aside all filthiness and overflow of wickedness, and receive with meekness the implanted word, which is able to save your souls. But be doers of the word and not hearers only, deceiving yourselves. For if anyone is a hearer of the word and not a doer, he is like a man observing his natural face in a mirror; for he observes himself, goes away, and immediately forgets what kind of man he was. But he who looks into the perfect law of liberty and continues in it, and is not a forgetful hearer but a doer of the work, this one will be blessed in what he does. (Jas. 1:18-25 NKJV)

Commit to Memory

Proverbs 3:5-6: ***Trust in the LORD with all your heart, and lean not on your own understanding; in all your ways acknowledge Him, and He will direct your paths.*** **(NKJV)**

God's Response to Obedience
(Part 3)

God will always respond favorably to us when we walk in obedience to His commands. He wants us to follow His commands because He truly knows what's best for us. Although walking in obedience to God will sometimes cause us some discomfort and pain (Hos. 1:2-3; 3:1-4), His purpose is to protect us from dangers that are usually unseen. Regardless of what temporary discomfort we might experience as a result of walking in obedience, we must always remember that God is sovereign and omniscient. He loves each of us dearly and has blessed us with every spiritual blessing (Eph. 1:3 -7).

God promised to provide the good of the land to those who walk in obedience and not to inflict them with plagues (Isa. 1:19; Exod. 15:24-26). We will suffer some trials as our Lord did (Rom. 8:13-17; 2 Tim. 3:12); however, because he already suffered, we can seek Him in time of need, and He will help us in our struggles and strong temptations (Heb. 2:14-18). Obedience to the Word of God is the powerful force that sets us free from the chains of sin and destruction (James 1:22-25). Jesus Christ is the key to a life of freedom from the intoxicating power of sin, which teases our flesh (Mark 8:31-36).

Man's idea of greatness and power is displayed by his desire to attain as many titles and worldly goods as he can possibly possess. His ways and ideas are totally contrary to that of the sovereign Creator of the universe (Isa. 55:8-9). God equates greatness with humility and obedience, not personal accomplishments and desires (Matt.18:1-4). It's not uncommon to find ourselves struggling to obey God when our desires are for things other than Him. The only way to walk in obedience to Him is make Him the object of our desire—putting God first above all things. Our flesh will dominate us if our hearts don't belong to God (Matt. 6:21-24).

We must begin to pray daily to the LORD to create in us a clean heart, to renew a right spirit within us, and to cleanse us from all unrighteousness. He promised that if we confess our sins, He will forgive us and cleanse us from all unrighteousness (1 John 1:9). There is no human way for us to win the battles we fight against our own flesh, the devil, and the world if we don't have the help of God almighty. We must always be mindful that we are engaged in spiritual warfare (Eph. 6:12-18); the devil wants to steal all that God has prepared for us and then kill every one of us (John 10:7-10).

However, as long as we walk in obedience to God, the devil can't harm us. He cannot even come against us without God's permission (Isa. 54:17; Job 1:6-12). God promised to bless all who are obedient to His Word. Throughout the Bible there are numerous examples of those who received God's blessings as a result of their obedience to His commands. From Abraham to Joshua to the apostles and all those in between (there are far too many to list), they were all recipients of God's blessings because of their obedience to Him. More than anything else, God desires a compassionate heart that leads to obedience—not sacrifice, works, or religious traditions (1 Sam. 15:20-23; Matt. 12:1-8).

If you are not currently walking in obedience to God, confess and pray. Begin your new life of obedience right now! Don't hesitate, because tomorrow is not promised to any of us. But watch how He responds to you.

Meditate on These Scriptures

> The speech pleased the LORD, that Solomon had asked this thing. Then God said to him: "Because you have asked this thing, and have not asked long life for yourself, nor have asked riches for yourself, nor have asked the life of your enemies, but have asked for yourself understanding to discern justice, behold, I have done according to your words; see, I have given you a wise and understanding heart, so that there has not been anyone like you before you, nor shall any like you arise after you. And I have also given you what you have not asked: both riches and honor, so that there shall not be anyone like you among the kings all your days. So if you walk in my ways, to keep My statutes and My commandments, as your father David walked, then I will lengthen your days."
>
> Then Solomon awoke; and indeed it had been a dream. And he came to Jerusalem and stood before the ark of the covenant of the LORD, offered up burnt offerings, offered peace offerings, and made a feast for all his servants. (1 Kings 3:10-15 NKJV)

> There was famine in the land, besides the first famine that was in the days of Abraham. And Isaac went to Abimelech king of the Philistines, in Gerar. Then the LORD appeared to him and said: "Do not go down to Egypt; live in the land of which I shall tell you. Dwell in this land, and I will be with you and bless you;

for to you and your descendants I give all of these lands, and I will perform the oath which I swore to Abraham your father. And I will make your descendants multiply as the stars of heaven; I will give to your descendants all these lands; and in your seed all the nations of the earth shall be blessed; because Abraham obeyed My voice and kept My charge, My commandments, My statutes, and My laws." So Isaac dwelt in Gerar. (Gen. 26:1-6 NKJV)

Commit to Memory

Psalm 34:7: ***The angel of the LORD encamps all around those who fear Him, and delivers them.*** **(NKJV)**

17

Making the Right Choices

Making the right choices in life is extremely important in the life of all Christians. Making the wrong choices can severely affect our service in ministry and our commitment to God. Our choices will determine our success in the spiritual world, as well as in the natural world—at least for a period. Making the right choices will protect us from unnecessary heartache and pain. Bad choices can be lasting and devastating! We are to always use the example given to us in the Bible as instruction for all our decision making, regardless of how important or unimportant the decision may be to us.

The first thing we must do is take a good look at some examples of the bad choices that were made by the servants of God and the results that followed. Adam's choice to obey Eve changed the entire world (Gen. 3:16-19). Abraham's choice to follow his wife's instructions and have relations with Hagar is still affecting the world today (Gen. 16:1-12; the battle still rages between the heirs). David chose to sleep with Bathsheba, and his entire household suffered the consequences (2 Sam. 11:1-5; 12:7-12). Our bad choices often will hurt others. Judas betrayed Jesus for thirty pieces of silver and suffered eternal damnation (Matt. 26:14-25).

The ability to make good choices is determined by our obedience to the Word of God. It is as simple as doing what the Bible says. The Bible gives us the answers to some of the most important choices that we will have to make in life. When we are choosing a mate (Prov. 3:5-6; 1 John 4:1), we should not just make our decision based on appearance or worldly success. When choosing a career (Prov. 3:5-6; Isa. 48:17), we should always consider what our skills and talents are before we make a final decision. When choosing those we want to be our friends and associates (1 Cor. 15:33; 2 Cor. 6:14), we must consider their beliefs.

Our choices will always be governed by the principle of sowing and reaping. If we make good choices, we will almost always reap positive results; but if we make bad choices that are contrary to the principles of the Bible, we will always reap negative results. Even in our bad choices, God is merciful; however, He will never change His principles. If we make choices without first seeking Him, we will suffer the consequences (Gal. 6:7). Even after we repent, we will still have to reap what we have sowed. Look at the example of King David; Israel still suffered after David repented of his sin (2 Sam. 24:1-16).

If we've made a bad choice in our life that is lasting (e.g., marriage, career, etc.), we must remember to continue to follow the principles of the Bible regardless of how difficult our situation may be. No matter what the situation is, we must pray daily and remain faithful and obedient to God, waiting on His deliverance (Ps. 55:22; 1 Cor.7:10-16). However, we should by all means do what we can to improve our present situation, as long as we're being obedient to God. The Bible says that God will cause all things to work together for our good (Rom. 8:28), however, we are not advised when or how it will take place.

We must change our old way of thinking and begin to search the Word of God (the Bible) for direction in all of our decision making. So instead of struggling to figure out what your choice should be, let God make it for, and you will not be disappointed. The Bible promises us that God will direct our path if we acknowledge Him in all of our ways.

This is the key to making good choices. We will always have a choice, but every choice is not always the best choice. Acknowledge God first, allow Him to direct your path, and He will help you make the best choice.

Meditate on These Scriptures

"I call heaven and earth as witnesses today against you, that I have set before you life and death, blessing and cursing; therefore choose life, that both you and your descendants may live; that you may love the LORD your God, that you may obey His voice, and that you may cling to Him, for He is your life and the length of your days; and that you may dwell in the land which the LORD swore to your fathers, Abraham, Isaac, and Jacob, to give to them." (Deut. 30:19-20 NKJV)

"Now therefore, fear the LORD, serve Him in sincerity and in truth, and put away the gods which your fathers served on the other side of the River and in Egypt. Serve the LORD! And if it seems evil to you to serve the LORD, choose for yourselves this day whom you will serve, whether the gods which your fathers served that were on the other side of the River, or the gods of the Amorites, in whose land you will dwell. But as for me and my house, we will serve the LORD." (Josh. 24:14-15 NKJV)

Commit to Memory

Romans 8:28: ***And we know that all things work together for good to those who love God, to those who are called according to His purpose.*** **(NKJV)**

18

Servants of God

In this present age, there is so much emphasis put on those in the body (church) who have titles or are in positions of leadership that the responsibility of the layperson goes unattended. We often do nothing because we expect someone else to do it. As followers of Jesus Christ, we have been given a mandate by our Lord to spread the gospel and make disciples (Matt. 28:18-20). Unfortunately, many of us rely on the leaders or ministers of the church to carry out the responsibilities that belong to us. All believers in Christ should render some extent of service to the body of Christ (the church).

To minister simply means to tend to the needs of others. A minister is a servant of God and all mankind (even those who are lost, for our testimony can lead them to Christ). Often we get so mesmerized by church titles that we forget what our responsibilities are as followers of Jesus Christ. Whether we have been ordained or licensed by the church or not, we still have a responsibility to spread the gospel and offer prayers and help to those in need. God has blessed each one of us individually with spiritual gifts and talents.

However, the Lord's commission was not just intended for a select few. He commissioned each of us (Matt. 28:18-20).

We were not all intended to be preachers or evangelists, but we all have a testimony to share. Each of us has his or her own testimony of how God has delivered us from total darkness and into the glorious kingdom of His dear Son. Our personal stories may not reach and deliver everyone who hears them, but they most certainly will reach and deliver some who hear them when they are mixed with the Word of God. Until we begin to step out from our comfort zone and dependency on others, we will never operate fully in the gifts and talents that our heavenly Father has bestowed upon us.

As we examine our service for God and what it means to be a servant of God, I think it will really benefit us to look at some of the offices (pastor, elder, minister, and deacon) held in the church and their biblical definitions.

Pastor – "the feeder, protector, and guide, or shepherd, of a flock of God's people in New Testament times. In speaking of spiritual gifts, the apostle Paul wrote that Christ 'gave some to be apostles, some prophets, some evangelists, and some pastors and teachers' (Eph. 4:11). The term pastor by this time in church history had not yet become an official title. The term implied the nourishing of and caring for God's people" *(Nelson's Illustrated Dictionary of the Bible).*

Elder – one who holds an office below the pastor and ahead of all other ministry leaders in the church. The church elder is seasoned and apt to fill in for the pastor in the event that he is needed. The elders were in local church government in Jerusalem (Acts 11:30; 21:18). The elders also were present with the apostles in Jerusalem at the church council (Acts 15). Paul addressed the elders regarding his departure and their continuing work in the ministry (Acts 20:17-35).

Minister, Ministry – "a distinctive biblical idea that means, 'to serve' or 'servant.' In the Old Testament the word servant was used primarily for court servants (I K. 10:5; Est. 1:10). During the period between the Old and New Testaments, it came to be used in connection with ministering to the poor. This use of the word is close to the work of the seven in waiting on tables in the New Testament (Acts 6:1-7). In reality, all believers are 'ministers.' The apostle Paul urged true pastor-teachers to 'equip the saints' so they can minister to one another—Eph. 4:11,12 *(Nelson's Illustrated Dictionary of the Bible)*.

Deacon – "a servant or minister; an ordained lay officer in many Christian churches. The general concept of deacon as a servant of the church is well established in both the Bible and church history. But the exact nature of the office is hard to define, because of changing concepts and varying practices among church bodies through the centuries. Another problem is that the Bible passages associated with deacons are interpreted differently by various church groups. The term deacon occurs in only two passages in the NKJV (Phil. 1:1; I Ti. 3:8-13). But the Greek word *diakonos* from which it is taken is found 30 times.

"In most cases *diakonos* is translated as 'servant' rather than 'deacon.' In the Greek world, *diakonos* was used to describe the work of a servant—a person who waited on tables or ministered as a religious official" *(Nelson's Illustrated Dictionary of the Bible)*.

Every office in the church is important and has its own function and responsibility. We are to respect the office and officers of the church (they are appointed by God for us) and pray daily for them. However, God is no respecter of persons and has appointed each of us for service. Don't rely on anyone else to do what God is expecting of you. We are all servants of the new covenant (2 Cor. 3:4-6). Even our Savior, being equal with God the Father, came to serve and not be served (Mark 1:45), how much more is required of us. It is paramount that we take our service for God very seriously. Anyone who does not serve God with his/her whole heart displeases Him.

We cannot serve God halfheartedly (Rev. 3:15-18). We must make a decision to serve God wholeheartedly or just sit back, do nothing, and expect someone else to pray for us and to do what God desires of us. Consider this: we sin when we don't serve (James 4:17), and our lack of service will hurt us (Gal. 6:7). These are extremely important points that we must seriously consider. If we're Christians God has prepared us for service; we are more than conquerors in Christ (Rom. 8:37), His Spirit lives in us (John 14:15-18), and His angels protect us (Ps. 34:7). What else, then, does it mean to be a servant of God?

To be a servant of God means to put aside our own opinions and fears and try our very best to meet the needs of others. As servants of God, we are to always walk in wisdom (God's wisdom: living by biblical principles). It is very important that all Christians follow the proper order of ministry—God, family, service. Unfortunately, many of us make the mistake of trying to save the world while the adversary is destroying our own households. This doesn't mean that we should minimize our service; it simply means we must be sober and alert at all times. God requires and expects us to spread the gospel at every opportunity we get.

Let us begin to crucify ourselves with Christ so that we can serve God. Pray to God daily for wisdom, boldness, fulfillment of the fruit of the Spirit, and the opportunity to impact the lives of others. Remember, you must read and study the Word of God daily so that when the opportunity comes along, you will be well prepared to share the good news in confidence. If God's servants don't allow their lights to shine, darkness will prevail. Praise God for all his servants!

Meditate on These Scriptures

If you have any encouragement from being united with Christ, if any comfort from His love, if any fellowship with the Spirit, if any tenderness and compassion, then make my joy complete by being like-minded, having the same love, being one in spirit and purpose. Do nothing out of selfish ambition or vain conceit, but in humility consider others better than yourself. Each of you should not look only to your own interests, but also to the interests of others. Your attitude should be the same as that of Christ: Who being in very nature God, did not consider equality with God something to be grasped, but made Himself nothing, taking the very nature of a servant, being made in human likeness.

And being found in appearance as a man, He humbled Himself and became obedient to death—even death on a cross! Therefore God exalted Him to the highest place and gave Him the name that is above every name, that at the name of Jesus every knee should bow, in heaven and on earth and under the earth, and every tongue confess that Jesus Christ is Lord, to the glory of God the Father. (Phil. 2:1-11 NIV)

This is a faithful saying: If a man desires the position of a bishop, he desires a good work. A bishop then must be blameless, the husband of one wife, temperate, sober minded, of good behavior, hospitable, able to teach; not given to wine, not violent, not greedy for money, but gentle, not quarrelsome, not covetous; one who rules his own house well, having his children in submission with reverence (for if a man does not know how to rule his own house, how will he take care of the church of God?); not a novice, lest being puffed up with pride he fall into the same condemnation as the devil.

Moreover he must have a good testimony among those who are outside, lest he fall into reproach and the snare of the devil. Likewise deacons must be reverent not doubled-tongued, not given to much wine, not greedy for money, holding the mystery of the faith with a pure conscience. But let those also first be tested; then let them serve as deacons, being found blameless. Likewise, their wives must be reverent, not slanderers, temperate, faithful in all things. Let deacons be the husband of one wife, ruling their children and their own houses well. For those who have served well as deacons obtain for themselves a good standing and great boldness in the faith which is in Christ Jesus. (I Tim. 3:1-13 NKJV)

Commit to Memory

James 4:17: ***Anyone, then, who knows the good he ought to do and doesn't do it, sins.*** **(NIV)**

19

Spiritual Gifts (Tongues)

Spiritual Gifts – "special gifts bestowed by the Holy Spirit upon Christians for the purpose of building up the church" *(Nelson's Illustrated Dictionary of the Bible).*

Gift of Tongues – "the Spirit-given ability to speak in languages not known to the speaker or in an ecstatic language that could not normally be understood by the speaker or the hearers" *(Nelson's Illustrated Dictionary of the Bible).*

God, through His Holy Spirit, has given spiritual gifts individually to all believers for the edification of the church (1 Cor. 12:7). These gifts include the word of wisdom, the word of knowledge, faith, gifts of healings, working of miracles, prophecy, discerning of spirits, different kinds of tongues, and the interpreting of tongues (1 Cor. 12:8-11). However, to understand the working of these gifts, we must look at each one of these gifts separately. Because of the church's great interest in tongues, we will examine this gift first. If all of these gifts come from God, why is there such a fascination with the gift of tongues? To find the answer to this question, we must examine the origin of this great fascination.

The Origin Of The Pentecostal Church

The great fascination with speaking in tongues can be traced back to the beginning of the Pentecostal movement a century ago. The most prominent figure in this great Pentecostal movement was a thirty-one-year-old African American pastor named William Joseph Seymour, considered by many to be the cofounder of modern Pentecostalism. Pastor Seymour was born in Centerville, Louisiana on May 2, 1870. He encountered a man named Charles F. Parham in Houston, Texas in 1905 and embraced the Pentecostal doctrine. In February 1906 he was called to preach at a church in Los Angeles.

Parham was later locked out of the church because of its disagreement with his doctrine. On April 9, 1906, Pastor Seymour was asked to conduct a gospel meeting at the home of Mr. and Mrs. Asbery (216 Bonnie Brae). While at this meeting he was approached by Mr. Edward Lee, in whose home the pastor had been a guest. Mr. Lee had been sick and asked the pastor to pray for his healing and that he might receive the baptism of the Holy Spirit. As the pastor began to pray, Lee was healed and filled with the Holy Spirit and began to speak in other tongues. Later that evening seven more people were filled with Holy Spirit and also spoke in tongues.

However, Pastor Seymour was not filled with the Holy Spirit until late on the night of April 12. Shortly afterwards, word of these miraculous events began to travel through the community. People began to flock to the Asbery residence until there was no room for all the people. The ministry eventually was moved to a vacant building located at 312 Azusa Street. This building was formerly the African Methodist

Episcopal Church (AME) but had been vacant and was used to store construction materials. This building would become the location of the great Azusa Street Revival.

The revivals would typically start around 10 a.m. and would sometimes last until two or three the next morning.

While conducting these revivals, Pastor Seymour would kneel on his knees with his head between two milk crates for hours, praying for the power of the Holy Spirit to come. Men and women from all over the world traveled to Azusa Street to be filled with the Holy Spirit. Many were filled with Holy Spirit, spoke in new languages, and then went to foreign lands to evangelize in their new tongue. From Azusa Street, Pentecostalism began to spread rapidly around the world, becoming a major force in Christendom. Even prior to Azusa Street, the Holy Spirit manifested Himself through the speaking of tongues.

In 1901 a man named Agnes M. Ozman was baptized with the Holy Spirit and began to speak in tongues. In Topeka Kansas at the Bethel Bible School, which was founded by Charles Fox Parham, he and his students also were baptized with the Holy Spirit and spoke in tongues. He later closed his school and began conducting revival meetings throughout the Midwest. Parham was also the teacher of Pastor Seymour for a short while. All of these men and most Pentecostals believe the only evidence of being baptized with the Holy Spirit is speaking in tongues.

However, no one can predict how God through His Holy Spirit will minister to a person's heart once he or she is filled with or baptized in the Holy Spirit. Although we hear almost every so-called man and woman of God speaking in tongues, we must always be mindful that tongues is a spiritual gift, and we do not all have the same gift (1 Cor. 12:28-30). All spiritual gifts are from God; they can't be taught, learned, developed, or mimicked. They are not natural but supernatural (1 Cor. 12:4-7). There are some in the church today who believe that they can mimic the power of God by attempting to teach or perfect God's spiritual gifts or even by pretending they have a gift they really do not have. This is nonsense and an offense to the Holy Spirit.

Now that we understand the history of the Pentecostal Church, we should have a better understanding of why so many Christians today profess (pretend) to speak in tongues. This is simply an attempt to impress others and lead them to believe that they are more spiritual or spiritually gifted than those who hear them. It is also a result of bad teaching and the inability to properly understand the context of Scripture (or possibly the result of habit—bad habit). To better understand the use of this gift (or proper operation), it is very important that we observe some scriptural principles regarding the use and purpose of tongues.

1. The tongue must be interpreted (1 Cor. 14:27).
2. Tongues are not for church without an interpreter (1 Cor. 14:28).
3. Tongues are for unbelievers, not believers (1 Cor. 14:22).
4. Most people who fake tongues in public aim to glorify themselves (1 Cor. 14:4).
5. Tongues are actual languages (Acts 2:1-12).

Careful observation of these findings reveals that the origin of the fascination of the gift of tongues started with the Pentecostal movement. Because the apostles spoke in tongues on the Day of Pentecost, the founders of the Pentecostal Church sincerely believed that the only evidence of being filled with the Spirit was speaking in tongues. Scripture clearly states that tongues is a spiritual gift given by the Holy Spirit to whom He pleases (1 Cor. 12:10-11). This revelation is proof that only some believers have the gift. However, this certainly does not mean that those with the gift of tongues are the only believers who are filled with the Holy Spirit.

Spiritual gifts are given to believers only, and they are administered by the Holy Spirit for the edification of the body (the church) of Jesus Christ (1 Cor. 12:7). As a result of my personal experience throughout my years in ministry and because of the widespread use (and misuse) of this particular gift, I feel it is extremely important to examine this phenomenon that is sweeping through so many of our churches. I thought it was important to examine in some detail this gift and the possible origin of this great desire by so many to possess this Holy Spirit-given gift. I think this information is vital for our spiritual growth and understanding of the truth.

As we enter church assemblies and observe those who are in error, let us all pray to God that He will give them wisdom and revelation regarding His spiritual gifts.

Meditate on These Scriptures

> And when this sound occurred, the multitude came together, and were confused, because everyone heard them speak in his own language. Then they were all amazed and marveled, saying to one another, "Look, are not all these who speak Galileans? And how is it that we hear, each in our own language in which we were born? Parthians and Medes and Elamites, those dwelling in Mesopotamia, Judea and Cappadocia, Pontus and Asia, Phrygia and Pamphylia, Egypt and the parts of Libya adjoining Cyrene, visitors from Rome, both Jews and proselytes, Cretans and Arabs—we hear them speaking in our own tongues the wonderful works of God." (Acts 2:6-11 NKJV)

> There are, it may be, so many kinds of languages in the world, and none of them are without significance.

Therefore, if I do not know the meaning of the language, I shall be a foreigner to him who speaks, and he who speaks shall be a foreigner to me. Even so you, since you are zealous for spiritual gifts, let it be for the edification, of the church that you seek to excel. Therefore let him who speaks in a tongue pray that he may interpret. For if I pray in a tongue my spirit prays, but my understanding is unfruitful. What is the conclusion then? I will pray with the spirit, and I will also pray with the understanding.

I will sing with the spirit, and I will also sing with the understanding. Otherwise, if you bless with the spirit, how will he who occupies the space of the uninformed say "Amen" at your giving of thanks, since he does not understand what you say? For you indeed give thanks well, but the other side is not edified. (1 Cor. 14:10-17 NKJV)

Commit to Memory

Ephesians 2:10: ***For we are His workmanship, created in Christ Jesus for good works, which God prepared before hand that we should walk in them.*** **(NKJV)**

Spiritual Gifts (Interpretation of Tongues)

The gift of "interpretation of tongues" gives an individual the ability to explain or interpret a language previously unknown to him or her that is being spoken by someone else. This amazing Spirit-given gift is evidence to unbelievers of the power of God. When the unbeliever knows that the interpreter previously had no knowledge of the language that is being interpreted, the reality of the power of the indwelling of the Holy Spirit is revealed (Acts 2:5-12; 1 Cor. 14:20-25). An interpreter should always be present when the gift of tongues is in operation. Without an interpreter the speaker should interpret what is said (1 Cor. 14:13).

The tongue should always be interpreted or the tongues-speaker should remain silent (1 Cor. 14:27-28). Without the presence of an interpreter, the speaker of the tongue causes confusion to those who are present (1 Cor. 14:29-33). Although I truly believe that all spiritual gifts are still in operation today, this particular gift is one that is rarely seen. As stated previously, faith is the substance that enables God's power to operate in all Christians. Just reading the Bible is not enough; we must truly commit ourselves to Christ. This commitment to the Lord entails sacrificing. There will never be any success without sacrifice—not in the natural or spiritual world.

That means investing your time in prayer, studying the Bible, and buying all of the necessary aids to help you study God's Word: Bible dictionaries, concordances, commentaries, and as many Bible translations as you can find. The easiest way to accomplish this is to buy one item at a time, and eventually you will have all the necessary material to really study God's Word. Start your intensive studying today, and the God of all mankind will transform your mind like you've never imagined. Only then can you truly operate in the spiritual gift that God through His Holy Spirit has blessed you with.

Meditate on These Scriptures

> "And it shall come to pass afterward that I will pour out My Spirit on all flesh; Your sons and your daughters shall prophesy, your old men shall dream dreams, your young men shall see visions. And also on My menservants and on My maidservants I will pour out My Spirit in those days." (Joel 2:28-29 NKJV)

> Now, brothers, if I come to you and speak in tongues, what good will I be to you, unless I bring you some revelation or knowledge or prophecy or word of instruction? Even in the case of lifeless things that make sounds, such as the flute or harp, how will anyone know what tune is being played unless there is a distinction in the notes? Again, if the trumpet does not sound a clear call, who will get ready for battle? So it is with you. Unless you speak intelligible words with your tongue, how will anyone know what you are saying? You will be speaking into the air. (1 Cor. 14:6-9 NIV)

Commit to Memory

1 Corinthians 14:28: ***Tongues, then, are not a sign for believers but for unbelievers; prophecy, however, is a sign for believers, not unbelievers.*** **(NIV)**

Spiritual Gifts (Wisdom)

Wisdom – "ability to judge correctly and follow the best course of action, based on knowledge and understanding" *(Nelson's Illustrated Dictionary of the Bible).*

This spiritual gift is described as a "word of wisdom," indicating that it enables those who have received it to speak valuable and useful advice into the lives of others, based on knowledge and understanding. Throughout the Bible there are numerous examples of God, His servants, and our Lord and Savior Jesus Christ using the gift of a word of wisdom. God used a word of wisdom when He warned Adam regarding the forbidden fruit (Gen. 2:16-17); Joseph used the gift after interpreting Pharaoh's dream (Gen. 41:33-36); David used the gift when he charged Solomon regarding the throne (1 Kings 2:1-4); and our Savior used the gift when He warned His disciples regarding their lack of prayer (Matt. 26:41).

Wisdom is the source that makes knowledge useful. Knowledge is information. Although it is important, it must have wisdom to be effective. However, the gift of wisdom refers to a deeper understanding of the Word of God or doctrinal truth. This can be seen in the writing of the apostle

Paul (1 Cor. 2:6-16). This gift enables those who are blessed with it to repeatedly make good decisions and give good, solid instruction based on the principles of God's Holy Word. The Holy Spirit administers this gift, like all of the other spiritual gifts, for the edification of the church as He sees fit for each person individually (1 Cor. 12:8).

Those whom the Holy Spirit has blessed with the gift of wisdom are well equipped to be wonderful advisers, counselors, and leaders. Wisdom is so very important because with it we can make decisions and choices that are pleasing to God. It also enables us to give advice that is useful and even life changing. Every Christian needs wisdom, but we will not all be blessed with the gift of wisdom. Nevertheless, if we study God's Word on a daily basis and pray for wisdom, the Holy Spirit will enlighten our understanding. This enlightenment will enable us to apply the principles of Scripture to our lives, leading to wise decisions and choices.

The Word of God is the very source that produces the wisdom that leads us to salvation, spiritual growth, and preparation (2 Tim. 3:15-17). God made it possible that we can all receive wisdom if we ask Him in faith (James 1:5-8). True wisdom will be shown in our good character and deeds, fueled by humility and reverence for God. True wisdom comes from above and is contrary to the natural wisdom of the world, which seeks its own gratification (James 3:13-18). Wisdom is a necessary and effective tool for all Christians. The wisdom needed to be effective in our daily walk with God is available to all who ask of God in faith.

The Bible says, "If any of you lacks wisdom, let him ask of God who gives freely without any finding of fault" (James 1:5). To impact the lives of others, we need to be equipped with wisdom from God. Godly wisdom will enable us to effectively advise and counsel those we encounter on a daily basis. The wisdom that comes from the Word of God is unlike the wisdom from the world, which is based on human knowledge

Because we know that all of us will not receive the gift of a "word of wisdom," let us pray daily to God for the necessary wisdom to be more effective in our daily Christian walk. Consider the prayer of the apostle Paul for the saints in Ephesus that they would receive the spirit of wisdom and revelation in the knowledge of God the Father (Eph. 1:15-23).

Consider also the wisdom of Solomon. When he could have asked God for anything and received it, he asked for wisdom, and God made him the wisest man to ever walk the earth (excluding Jesus Christ, who was fully man and fully God). Because his request was pleasing to God, God blessed Solomon with materials things also (1 Kings 3:7-12).

Meditate on These Scriptures

> The LORD by wisdom founded the earth; by understanding He established the heavens; By His knowledge the depths were broken up, and the clouds drop down the dew. (Prov. 3:19-20 NKJV)

> Happy is the man who finds wisdom, and the man who gains understanding; for her proceeds are better than the profile of silver, and her gain than fine gold. She is more precious than rubies, and all the things you may desire cannot compare to her. Length of days is in her right hand, in her left hand riches and honor. Her ways are ways of pleasantness, and all her paths are peace. She is a tree of life to those who take hold of her, and happy are all who retain her. (Prov. 3:13-18 NKJV)

Commit to Memory

Proverbs 2:6: ***For the LORD gives wisdom; From His mouth come knowledge and understanding.*** **(NKJV)**

Spiritual Gifts (A Word of Knowledge)

Knowledge – "the truth or facts of life that a person acquires either through experience or thought. The greatest truth that a person can possess with the mind or learn through experience is truth about God" *(Nelson's Illustrated Dictionary of the Bible).*

Knowledge in the natural sense is information based on fact. However, the gift of knowledge is the ability to apply doctrinal truth to everyday life situations. This gift is described as "a word of knowledge" (1 Cor. 12:8), indicating the gift is active and far more than just the ability to interpret Scripture. The gift enables those who have it to offer the Word of God to others in situations when most of us would falter (lean on our own understanding). It is a supernatural gift like the others and cannot be mimicked. Throughout the Bible there are numerous examples of God's servants using the gift.

The apostle Paul exercised the gift of a word of knowledge (1 Cor. 6:19; 11:2-3); the apostle Peter exercised the gift of a word of knowledge (Acts 2:38; 16:31); James, the brother of our Lord and Savior Jesus Christ, exercised the gift of a word of knowledge (James 1:5-8; 2:17-20); and the

Lord exercised the gift of a word of knowledge too many times to list (e.g., Matt. 4:1-11; Mark 6:3-6; Luke 5:4-10). This gift, like the others, is intended for the edification of the body of Christ (the church). When this gift is in operation, it has the ability to redirect lives that the devil may have knocked off track.

The gift of knowledge gives the ability to offer powerful and encouraging words inspired by God when they are needed the most. This unique ability is a life changer. Those who possess the gift of knowledge will always be recognized for their reverence for God. The Bible says, "The fear of the LORD is the beginning of knowledge, but fools despise wisdom and discipline" (Prov. 1:7 NIV). The Hebrew word for fool in the Old Testament describes one who is morally deficient. If we don't reverence the LORD, we're morally deficient. Those who are blessed with the gift of knowledge are morally sufficient.

Knowledge can be attained from reading and studying the Bible on a daily basis. The first step to getting knowledge is a venerating, honoring, and esteeming awe of the LORD. To earn knowledge, we must learn of God, and this can be achieved only by studying the Bible. The Bible says, "For the LORD gives wisdom; from His mouth come knowledge and understanding" (Prov. 2:6 NKJV). God speaks to us through His Word (the Bible); for this reason, we must study the Bible daily to know what God desires of us and to understand His ways. Just as He made known His ways unto Moses, He will reveal Himself to us through His Word.

The knowledge we attain from studying the Bible will reveal God's loving and merciful character to us. Here are some important things that we will learn about our heavenly Father as we study His Word: He protects and provides for those who fear Him (Ps. 34:7-9), He heals those who fear His name (Mal. 4:2), He is merciful to those who fear Him (Luke

1:49-50), and He will supply all of our needs according to His riches and glory in Christ Jesus (Phil. 4:19).

Pray daily that God will bless you with wisdom, knowledge, and understanding. Although we will not all receive the gift of a word of knowledge, if we ask in faith, He will increase our wisdom (James 1:5-8), and studying the Bible daily will increase and develop our knowledge.

Meditate on These Scriptures

> My son, if you receive my words, and treasure my commands within you, so that you incline your ear to wisdom, and apply your heart to understanding; Yes, if you cry out for discernment, and lift up your voice for understanding, if you seek her as silver, and search for her as for hidden treasures; Then you will understand the fear of the LORD, and find the knowledge of God. (Prov. 2:1-5 NKJV)

> My son, pay attention to my wisdom; Lend your ear to my understanding, that you may preserve discretion, and your lips may keep knowledge. (Prov. 5:1-2 NKJV)

Commit to Memory

Proverbs 1:7: ***The fear of the LORD is the beginning of knowledge, but fools despise wisdom and instruction.*** **(NKJV)**

Spiritual Gifts (Faith)

"Faith is the assurance (the confirmation, the title deed) of things we hope for, being the proof of things we do not see and the conviction of their reality (faith perceiving as real fact what is not revealed to the senses)" (Heb. 11:1 Amplified Bible). Faith is obeying, believing, trusting, and relying totally upon God for all of our needs, whether spiritual or natural. The gift of faith is from the Holy Spirit; however, there are three different types or levels of faith that exist in the world: natural faith, saving faith, and the gift of faith.

Natural Faith – We are all born with this type of faith. An example of natural faith is sitting in a chair with no concern for whether or not the chair will hold us, or turning on a light switch and fully expecting the light to come on. These things we do naturally without any question.

Saving Faith – This type of faith is what could be described as elementary faith. It is the faith to believe God for salvation (faith to be saved through the Word of God; Rom. 10:9-10).

The Gift of Faith – This type of faith is a spiritual gift that is given by the Holy Spirit to whomever He pleases. Not everyone will have this kind of faith (1 Cor. 12:9a). This kind of faith can be seen in the life of Jesus Christ, the apostles, many of the prophets, and the patriarch Abraham. Even those of us who have not received the gift of faith can still walk in power by believing and trusting wholly in God without doubting (Matt. 21:18-21). The gift of faith is not like ordinary faith; it is a supernatural faith that enables those who have the gift to believe God and His Word, even in situations that appear impossible (Heb. 11:12).

Even great faith is tested, tried, and even stretched to its fullest limits by God in order that it may grow even more. Abraham had to wait 24 years before he could receive the promise—the birth of his son Isaac. He was 100 years old and Sarah 90 years old when Isaac was born (Gen. 17:1-4; 21:1-5). Although everyone doesn't have the gift of faith, we all have been appointed a measure of faith (Rom. 12:3). This measure of faith will increase if our lives are totally dedicated to God or remain stagnant if we attempt to serve Him half-heartedly. Here are five points that help our faith to grow.

- We must study the Word of God daily.
- We must continually apply the Bible's principles to our lives.
- We must pray morning, noon, and night (pray the Holy Spirit will enlighten us).
- We must learn God's promises and believe them for our lives.
- Most importantly, we must be obedient to the Word of God.

Faith and obedience are inseparable; it's impossible to be disobedient to the Word of God and walk in faith at the same time. Our level of obedience will reveal our level of faith. If we believe God, we will be obedient to the entire Bible regardless of our circumstances, and our faith and obedience will assure our righteousness (right standing or proper relationship with God). Noah obeyed God and became an heir of righteousness (Heb. 11:7). Abraham obeyed God, and it was credited to him as righteousness (Heb. 11:8). Our obedience is equivalent to faith and amounts to righteousness with God. If our faith is little and not growing, let us examine our obedience to the Word of God. We must examine our lives to find out what area(s) where we are lacking in obedience. If we can identify where we are walking in disobedience and correct it, our faith will begin to grow.

By faith Abraham offered up Isaac (Heb. 11:17-19), much as God sent His only begotten Son into the world. Meditate on this: Love for God exemplifies faith.

Meditate on These Scriptures

> But without faith it is impossible to please Him, for he who comes to God must believe that He is, and that He is a rewarder of those who diligently seek Him. (Heb. 11:6 NKJV)

> By faith Moses, when he became of age, refused to be called the son of Pharaoh's daughter, choosing rather to suffer affliction with the people of God than to enjoy the passing pleasure of sin, esteeming the reproach of Christ greater riches than the treasures in Egypt; for he looked to the reward. (Heb. 11:24-26 NKJV)

Commit to Memory

Romans 1:17: *For in it the righteousness of God is revealed from faith to faith; as it is written, "The just shall live by faith."* **(NKJV)**

Spiritual Gifts (Gifts of Healings)

Gift of Healing – "the ability to restore health and hold off death for a temporary period of time" *(Bible Knowledge Commentary: New Testament)*.

This gift is described in the Bible as gifts of healings or gifts of healing—it varies depending on the Bible translation (1 Cor. 12:9 NKJV, KJV, NIV, etc). Although it is one gift, it is noted in the plural form, implying that this gift effectively operates in different ways to bring about restoration of health or bodily functions from numerous types of ills or sicknesses. It also implies that this gift is continuously working—it is not a one-time experience. Like the other gifts, it cannot be taught or mimicked. Throughout the New Testament, there are numerous examples of the Lord and His disciples using this awesome gift.

The gift of healing is closely associated with faith—in both the individual receiving the healing and the individual operating the gift. Many who have the gift of healing lack the faith to exercise the gift. Because of this lack of faith, they never operate in this awesome manifestation of the Holy Spirit that resides in them. Pride and fear hinder their faith because they're generally afraid of failing in front of people. This is simply a lack of trust in God. Because of this fear, they will never attempt to use the gift. Therefore, they will never know if they have been blessed with this extraordinary gift.

The apostles could not heal the boy with epilepsy because they lacked the necessary faith (Matt. 17:14-20). The apostles probably could not heal the boy because they looked at the severity of his condition instead of the power of God. Interestingly, Jesus stated their lack of faith impeded their power and that some (demons) come out only by prayer and fasting (Matt. 17:21). (Note that this occurred before the apostles were filled with Holy Spirit [Acts 2:1-4]. As we know from the New Testament, once the apostles were filled with the Holy Spirit, they performed many signs and wonders, founded the church, and spread the gospel throughout the world.)

Although the Holy Spirit distributes spiritual gifts as He sees fit without any works or requirements, faith is the substance that joins all things together in Christ. We must walk in faith to operate in our gifts and to be pleasing to God. On many occasions the Lord related the healing of someone to his/her faith (Jesus credits the faith of the sick to their healing in Matt. 9:20-22, 28-30). Apostle Paul discerned the faith of the lame man and healed him (Acts 14:8-10). The gift of healing is still in operation today (John 14:12-17; James 5:14-15). Unfortunately, very few have the necessary faith to exercise this gift.

One must truly believe God to step out on faith and attempt to heal the sick and lame (especially when others are present). This gift must be tested to prove it exists. Anyone who truly believes God has gifted him/her with this gift will attempt to heal the sick regardless of where he is or who else is present or the severity of the illness. If you believe that God through His Holy Spirit has blessed you with the gift of healing, pray that God will increase your faith and bless you with the necessary boldness to step out on faith and heal those who are sick. Do not be afraid or ashamed. Even the apostles prayed for boldness after they had already received the promise of the Holy Spirit (Acts 4:23-31).

Meditate on These Scriptures

> Is anyone among you suffering? Let him pray. Is anyone cheerful? Let him sing psalms. Is anyone among you sick? Let him call the elders of the church, and let them pray over him, anointing him with oil in the name of the Lord. And the prayer of faith will save the sick, and the Lord will raise him up. And if he has committed sins, he will be forgiven. Confess your trespasses to one another, and pray for one another, that you may be healed. The effective, fervent prayer of a righteous man avails much. (James 5:13-16 NKJV)

> As He went along, He saw a man blind from birth. His disciples asked Him, "Rabbi, who sinned, this man or his parents, that he was born blind." "Neither this man nor his parents sinned," said Jesus, "but this happened so that the work of God might be displayed in his life. As long as it is day, we must do the work of Him who sent Me. Night is coming, when no one can work. While I am in the world, I am the light of the world." Having said this, He spit on the ground, made some mud with the saliva, and put it on the man's eyes. "Go, He told him, wash in the pool Siloam" (this word means Sent). So the man went and washed, and came home seeing. (John 9:1-6 NIV)

Commit to Memory

John 14:15: ***"If you love Me, keep My commandments."*** **(NKJV)**

Spiritual Gifts (Working of Miracles)

Working of Miracles – the ability of a believer in Christ to perform phenomena that defy the laws of nature and logic, therefore revealing the presence and power of the Spirit of God.

When the gift of working of miracles is in operation, it is a powerful testimony of the omnipotence and omnipresence of the Almighty God. When God works miracles through His people, even those who don't believe must acknowledge Him. People know a true miracle when they see it. It is an unnatural act that very rarely occurs and has no natural explanation. What distinguishes the power of the working of miracles from a counterfeit is that it simply has no natural explanation. All spiritual gifts are for the edification of the church, but some have a greater ability to reach the lost (miracles, healings, tongues, interpreting tongues).

These particular spiritual gifts are outward gifts that have a dramatic visual effect on those who are present when they are in operation. If a miracle occurs in the presence of unbelievers—if a blind man receives his sight or salvation is preached in an unknown language by one whom everyone knows previously had no ability to speak that language and another who also previously lacked the ability interprets—those who are present will certainly know that the power of God is in operation, and many will receive Jesus Christ as their Savior. Yet this is by no means to say that the other gifts are less important.

The witness of the gift of miracles will draw the lost out of darkness and into God's marvelous light. Many believe after they witness the power of God through Christ (John 4:43-53), even those who oppose the gospel acknowledge the power of God (Acts 4:13-16), and the miraculous power of the gift expands the church (Acts 5:12-16). There is no denying that the above-mentioned gifts have a profound effect on those who are not saved when they witness these gifts in operation. The Bible says that some gifts are not for believers but for the benefit of nonbelievers that they might believe (1 Cor. 14:20-25).

The other gifts (wisdom, knowledge, faith, prophecy, and discernment) are no less powerful but are more geared to the edification and building up of those who are already a part of the body of Christ (the church). The church could not operate effectively without a wise leader. And without knowledgeable saints filled with discernment, it would be led astray. Without one who prophesies (proclaims and explains the Word of God), many would be without true understanding. And, of course, the church could not exist without the power of faith.

All spiritual gifts are important to the church. They are God's gifts to the church through His Holy Spirit for the edification of the entire church, for outreach and enlightenment of the lost, and for glorifying the living God. After the promise of the Holy Spirit was fulfilled at Pentecost (Acts 2:1-4), the founders of the church and their followers exercised all the spiritual gifts. It was the presence of the Holy Spirit that enabled the founders (apostles) of the early church to operate in the power promised by the Lord (Acts 1:4-8).

I am thoroughly convinced that in order for the church to operate in the power of the Holy Spirit, we must all return to total holiness.

We must examine our lives daily for any sign of iniquity and then repent and ask the Holy Spirit to vanquish it from our lives. We must also come together as one body in one accord. This is not an easy process, but the key is total humility. We must be willing to confess that apart from the Spirit of God we are totally wicked and lost. We must make a more valiant effort to study His Word and apply the principles of His Word to our lives and begin to embrace one another in love. This is a daily process that will take a lifelong effort. Although difficult, the fruits of this holy lifestyle are priceless. Only then will the church operate in the power of God and the gifts of the Holy Spirit

Meditate on These Scriptures

> Now both Jesus and His disciples were invited to the wedding. And when they ran out of wine, the mother of Jesus said to Him, " They have no wine." Jesus said to her, "Woman what does your concern have to do with Me? My hour has not yet come." His mother said to the servants, "Whatever He says to you, do it." Now there were set there six waterpots of stone, according to the manner of purification of the Jews, containing twenty or thirty gallons apiece. Jesus said to them, "Fill the waterpots with water." And they filled them up to the brim. And He said to them, "Draw some out now, and take it to the master of the feast."
>
> And they took it. When the master of the feast had tasted the water that was made wine, and did not know where it came from (but the servants who had drawn the water knew), the master of the feast called

the bridegroom. And he said to him, "Every man at the beginning sets out the good wine, and when the guests have well drunk, then the inferior. You have kept the good wine until now!" This beginning of signs Jesus did in Cana of Galilee, and manifested His glory; and His disciples believed in Him. (John 2:2-11 NKJV)

The apostles performed many miraculous signs and wonders among the people. And all the believers used to meet together in Solomon's Colonnade. No one else dared join them, even though they were highly regarded by the people. Nevertheless, more and more men and women believed in the Lord and were added to their number. As a result, people brought the sick into the streets and laid them on beds and mats so that at least Peter's shadow might fall on some of them as he passed by. (Acts 5:12-15 NKJV)

Commit to Memory

1 John 1:9: ***If we confess our sins, He is faithful and just and will forgive us of our sins and purify us from all unrighteousness.*** **(NIV)**

Spiritual Gifts (Prophecy)

Prophecy – "predictions about the future and the end-time; special messages from God, often uttered through human spokesman, which indicate the divine will for mankind on earth and in heaven" *(Nelson's Illustrated Dictionary of the Bible).*

To prophesy is to proclaim the Word of God or say what God says. The Old Testament prophets (also John the Baptist) received the message from God audibly (Gen. 6:13; Exod. 3:4; Jer. 1:4-5). However, today the message of the prophet comes directly from the spoken Word of God, the Bible (Rev. 22:18-19). This is simply because the canon (or Scripture) is complete. There will be nothing else added to the Word of God. Plainly speaking, to prophesy means to expound and interpret the written Word of God, not soothsaying or fortune-telling. Only God knows what the future holds, but by studying the Bible we can recognize the signs of the times.

The primary responsibility of the modern-day prophet is to provide guidance and edification to the church by expounding on the meaning of God's Word. This involves explaining the truth and revelation of Jesus Christ and

God the Father's promises and purpose for all of mankind directly from the Bible, not using one's personal opinion of someone's present state and what he/she believes the future holds for any particular person (Eph. 3:2-5). We must always be mindful that Jesus Christ is the source and fulfillment of all prophecy and prophetic truth (Gen. 3:14-15; Luke 24:25-27).

The gift of prophecy is intended to guide, instruct, and build up the listeners (1 Cor. 14:3). Prophecy illuminates the meaning of God's Word and reveals to the lost the need to be born again (1 Cor.14:24-25). To prophesy is not merely to tell people what you believe is some special message you have received from God for them. Such an idea comes from one who thinks he or she is superspiritual and has a special relationship with God. That is totally refuted by Scripture (Acts 10:34-35; Rom. 2:11; 10:12; Gal 2:6). The gift of prophecy is not a pseudo-psychic power given to anyone who wants it.

It is a spiritual gift given by the Holy Spirit to whom He sees fit (1 Cor. 12:11). Any communication that is said to be a message from God must come directly from the Bible or be founded 100 percent on biblical principles. Any message that is contrary to Scripture cannot be from God. We must learn to try every spirit and not allow ourselves to be deceived into believing that everything that is said is a personal message from God for us (1 John 4:1). Those whose prophetic word does not come to pass are not speaking from God (Deut 18:22). We must be mindful that oftentimes the message we receive from those who claim to be prophets is not a message from God.

These messages can be extremely harmful if we choose to follow them without first comparing their message with the Bible (Matt. 7:15-18; 2 Cor. 11:3-15; 2 Pet. 2:1-3). Never assume the message you receive from someone who claims to be blessed with the gift of prophecy is from God—especially if that message is said to be for you specifically. Pray and study the Bible daily so that false prophets will not misguide you. Walk in faith and obedience, and ask God to reveal to you if you have been blessed with the gift of prophecy.

Meditate on Theses Scriptures

"I will raise up for them a Prophet like you from among their brethren, and will put My words in His mouth, and He shall speak to them all that I command Him. And it shall be that whoever will not hear My words, which He speaks in My name, I will require of him. But the prophet who presumes to speak a word in My name, which I have not I have not commanded him to speak, or who speaks in the name of other gods, that prophet shall die. And if you say in your heart, "How shall we know the word which the LORD has not spoken?

When a prophet speaks in the name of the LORD, if the thing does not happen or come to pass, that is the thing which the LORD has not spoken; the prophet has spoken it presumptuously; you shall not be afraid of him." (Deut. 18:18-22 NKJV)

"But of that day and hour no man knows, not even the angels of heaven, but my Father only. But as the days of Noah were, so also will the coming of the Son of man be. For as in the days before the flood, they were eating and drinking, marrying and giving in marriage, until the day that Noah entered the ark, and did not know until the flood came and took them all away, so also will the coming of the Son of man be." (Matt. 24:36-39 NKJV)

Commit to Memory

Galatians 4:4-5: ***But when the fullness of time had come, God sent forth His Son, born of a woman, born under the law, to redeem those who were under the law, that we might receive the adoption as sons.*** **(NKJV)**

Spiritual Gifts (Discerning of Spirits)

"Discerning of spirits is a gift of the Holy Spirit, which enables a person to judge whether one who speaks in tongues or performs miracles does so by the power of the Holy Spirit or by a false spirit – I Co. 12:10" *(Nelson's Illustrated Dictionary of the Bible).*

The gift of discerning spirits is quite different from natural discernment because it makes its determinations based on the truths of God's Word, not opinions or personal experiences. Discernment reveals what spirit works in the prophet (Deut. 18:15-22; Christ the prophet). Discernment will also reveal selfish and false leaders who are not of God (Ezek. 34:2-4). This spiritual gift is usually prevalent in those who are called by God to lead a flock. After Pentecost the apostles used the gift of discernment: Peter discerned Simon's spirit (Acts 8:14-23), and Paul discerned the slave girl's spirit (Acts 16:16-18).

The Holy Spirit distributes different spiritual gifts to different Christians. However, even though we are not all gifted with spiritual discernment, we can all use the Word of God to discern the motives and intentions of people (Heb. 4:12). In our attempt to discern the spirit of an individual, it is always far more effective to listen than to talk. Listening will always reveal what's inside the heart (Matt. 12:34-35). We will also be able to discern the heart of an individual by his/her actions (Matt. 6:19-21). Those who sow primarily to spiritual things are of God, in contrast to those who sow primarily to the things of this world.

Discernment is essential in our Christian walk. We must be discerning so that false prophets, bad doctrine, and deceiving spirits do not lead us astray. Following bad doctrine and bad spiritual advice will not only hinder our spiritual growth; it will also destroy our testimony. The inability to discern spirits can even endanger our lives. The Lord said, "The thief does not come except to steal, and kill, and to destroy" (John 10:10a). He also takes advantage of every opportunity to deceive the children of God. Even from the beginning, he was the world's greatest deceiver and liar (Gen. 3:1-7).

However, using the Word of God as a barometer to determine the truth from a lie is the key to developing discernment and dispelling deception (1 John 2:18-22). The importance of following the principles of the Bible and the teaching of our Savior Jesus Christ is no more evident than in Lord's statement regarding the end times: "For false christs and false prophets will rise and show great signs and wonders to deceive, if possible, even the elect" (Matt. 24:24). His statement truly reveals the deceiving powers of Satan and his cohorts. We must always test people by the Word of God and not assume that they are of God just because they have talent, charisma, or a title.

The Bible clearly states that we are to test every spirit (1 John 4:1-4). This will never be an easy or quick process, but it will prevent us from being deceived and misled. We must exercise patience in the process of discerning spirits, as we allow the Word of God to reveal to us what type of spirit controls an individual. The Bible is the most efficient source for examining character, motive, and spiritual truth. It is truly the inspired Word of God (2 Tim. 3:16) and the only source we need for discerning spirits without the gift of discernment. I Thank God for the gifts He has given to His church along with His Word, which enable us to discern the truth from falsehood.

Meditate on These Scriptures

> There are diversities of gifts, but the same Spirit. There are differences of ministries, but the same Lord. And there are diversities of activities, but it is the same God who works all in all. The manifestation of the Spirit is given to each one for the profit of all: for one is given the word of wisdom through the Spirit, to another the word of knowledge through the same Spirit, to another faith by the same Spirit, to another gifts of healings by the same Spirit, to another the working of miracles by the same Spirit, to another prophecy, to another discerning of spirits, to another different kinds of tongues, to another the interpretation of tongues.
>
> But and the same Spirit works all these things, distributing to each one individually as He wills. (1 Cor. 12:4-11 NKJV)

> Love never fails. But whether there are prophecies, they will fail; whether there are tongues, they will cease; whether there is knowledge, it will vanish away. For we know in part and we prophesy in part. But when that which is perfect has come, then that which is in part will be done away. When I was a child, I spoke as a child, I understood as a child, I thought as a child; but when I became a man, I put

away childish things. For now we see in a mirror, dimly, but then face to face.

Now I know in part, but then I shall know just as I also am known. And now abide faith, hope, love, these three; but the greatest of these is love. (1 Cor. 12:8-13 NKJV)

Commit to Memory

Hebrews 4:12: ***For the word of God is living and powerful, and sharper than any two – edged sword, piercing even to the division of soul and spirit, and joints and marrow, and is a discerner of the thoughts and intents of the heart.*** **(NKJV)**

20

Holiness and the Crucified Life (Part 1)

Holiness, Godliness – walking in total obedience to the commands and principles of the Bible; a life modeled after the life of Jesus Christ. Walking in holiness also can be defined as living a life in total submission to God. This type of lifestyle is not a choice; it is a command from God to all Christians (1 Pet. 1:13-16). There are no levels or periods of holiness; we are either living in holiness—submission and obedience to the Word of God—or we are living in rebellion, which is sin (Matt. 6:24; Rom. 6:16). The fruit that our lives produce is a direct measure of our holiness. If we are walking in holiness, our example will impact the lives of others.

There is no better measure of holiness than our own homes. If we are truly walking in holiness, it will have a profound effect on our families. Our witness of a life guided by holiness is the best instruction for our children, spouses, and siblings. Our steadfast commitment to Jesus Christ will reveal to those of our households the character and love of God. On the contrary, if we profess Christ but live as those who are unsaved, we make ourselves to be a living lie. This hypocritical, compromising character is the worse example of anyone who considers himself/herself to be a Christian. It is this behavior that misguides the weak.

Our unspoken testimony is far more important than many of us even realize. There is an old saying that says, "Someone is always watching." This is the motto we as Christians must live by. Those who reject the gospel of Jesus Christ are always waiting for an opportunity to catch us in compromising positions. Once they do, they will use this to challenge our Christian faith and character. As ambassadors of the Lord and heirs of God's promises, we must always positively represent Him who gave so much for us.

Jesus said that we are the salt and light of this world (Matt.5:14-16). That's more evidence of the importance of a life of holiness lived in clear view for the whole world to see. God wants us to live our lives out loud. In other words, our lifestyle and character should minister to others without a word being spoken from our mouths. Holiness is not a work in progress; it is a decision to honor God in all that we do. This decision to honor God requires some sacrifice and a commitment to God. Our sacrifice entails exercising self-denial and committing our lives to the things that honor and glorify God. Some of these things include volunteering our time and services to those in need and spreading the gospel when possible.

Holiness and the crucified life are synonymous. It's impossible to walk in holiness without living the crucified life. Living the crucified life literally means death to our old nature and a life totally committed to Jesus Christ (Gal. 2:20). Living a crucified, holy life means understanding that just because we can, doesn't mean that we should, and that everything that looks good to us, isn't necessarily good for us. Eve saw that the forbidden fruit was desirable and chose to eat it—the rest is history. When we truly become crucified with Christ, our strong desires will no longer have control over our actions.

Our examples of living the crucified, holy life should come from Scripture. The Bible shows us how God empowers those who serve Him with the ability to live the crucified life of holiness. The Lord exemplified the crucified life of holiness with humility and total obedience to the Father (Phil 2:5-8); after his conversion, the apostle Paul lived a crucified, holy life (Phil 3:4-11); and Joseph was able to resist the temptations of the flesh because he honored and reverenced the living God of his father (Gen. 39:7-10). He was an excellent example of one who lived a life of holiness.).

Obedience, sacrifice, and humility comprise the life of holiness. Without adapting our lives to these three important factors, we will never succeed in living a life of holiness. Let us pray daily that God will break our pride and create in us a clean heart and a renewed spirit (Ps. 51:10). Let's also be mindful that we must always pray for the entire body of Christ—that we will all be of one accord, united in Him, to serve the mighty God and Father of our Savior Jesus Christ. Let us begin at this very moment to live a life of holiness while there is still time, for we know that those who do not live a life of holiness will not see the Lord (Heb. 12:14-16).

Meditate on These Scriptures

> As a prisoner of the Lord, then, I urge you to live a life worthy of the calling you have received. Be completely humble and gentle; be patient, bearing with one another in love. Make every effort to keep the unity of the Spirit through the bond of peace. (Eph. 4:1-3 NIV)

> Live in harmony with one another. Do not be proud, but be willing to associate with people of low position. Do not be conceited. Do not repay anyone evil for evil. Be careful to do what is right in the eyes

of everybody. If it is possible, as far as it depends on you, live at peace with everyone. Do not take revenge, my friends, but leave room for God's wrath for it is written: "It is mine to avenge; I will repay," says the Lord. On the contrary: "If your enemy is hungry, feed him; "If he is thirsty, give him something to drink. In doing this, you will heap burning coals on his head." Do not be overcome by evil, but overcome evil with good. (Rom. 12:16-21 NIV)

Commit to Memory

1 Peter 1:16: ***For it is written: "Be holy, because I am Holy."*****(NIV)**

Holiness And The Crucified Life
(Part 2)

To live a crucified holy life, we must first learn to humble ourselves. Once we have learned to humble ourselves, we must be willing to submit ourselves to others as unto God. It is extremely important that we understand what submitting as unto God means. This powerful expression simply means as we submit to the individual God has placed in headship over us, we are actually submitting to God out of obedience to His spoken Word and not just to the individual, whether it be our spouse, boss, or spiritual leader—pastor, elder, etc (Eph. 5:22,23; Heb. 13:17; 1 Pet. 2:13-16).

The Bible says, "Wives, likewise, . . . be submissive to your own husbands" (1 Pet. 3:1a). However, many women don't submit because of their desire for headship (to rule over their husbands). Much of this behavior is the result of a lack of a strong Christian male presence in their childhood. Without that strong presence in the early stages of life, many women have adopted a mind-set that men were not intended to be the head of the household because they can survive just fine with or without him. The lack of a strong male (Christian male) presence affects men as well as women. Many of the problems in marriages stem from the man's inability to be the head of the household because he himself never had an example to learn from.

Therefore a struggle ensues between the two for the role God appointed to the man. Man was intended to be the head of woman, as Christ is the head of man (Eph. 5:22-25; this does not mean man rules over the woman). This struggle between the two places both man and woman in sin and damages their communication with the God of their salvation (1 Pet. 3:7-12). God created both equally and for each other's benefit. However, it was His intention that the man should have headship in the home and the church.

Sadly, many women get this confused and in turn refuse to obey God and submit. Notice the Bible says, "Wives submit to your own husbands, as to the Lord" (Eph. 5:22). This means your submission is to Christ through your husband. On the other hand, far too many men misunderstand what it means to be the head. Before we pound our chests, men, we must understand that being the head means providing your wife with everything she needs, and I'm not just referring to material things. The Bible also says that the husband should love his wife as Christ loved the church.

Can we even fathom what that really means? First, we must understand that the Lord's sacrifice for the church was the greatest sacrifice known to man. There has never been, nor will there ever be a sacrifice like His. Now that's how we are to love our wives! Being the head means supplying their needs before they ask. If man's only responsibility was primarily supplying his wife with material things that would be easy. However, God expects the husband to spiritually nourish and support his wife in everything, just as Christ did for His body (the church). Now, the question is, how many of us are fulfilling these requirements?

I wish I could honestly say that I was, but as a man of God I must be truthful. I push toward the mark of His higher calling, but in this obligation I often fall short. Nonetheless,

I continue to strive to please God and sufficiently satisfy my wife. In our submission in marriage (men also submitting to the needs of our wives physically, emotionally, and spiritually), we honor God and exemplify the crucified, holy life.

Many of us miss our blessings because we refuse to submit to the authority (supervisor, boss, etc.) figure at our workplace. This type of behavior is rebellious and a sin against God, not just the boss (1 Pet. 2:18-21). This will eventually cause us to harbor malice in our hearts and destroy our ability to walk in holiness and live the crucified life (Ps. 66:18). This mind-set represents a prideful heart that will prevent us from growing spiritually. Unfortunately, too many men and women of God are in prisons (even one is too many) because of their inability to control their greed and fleshly desires. They break the laws of both God and man and eventually pay the price (Rom. 13:1-7; Gal. 6:7).

To live a crucified life, we must become disciples (pupils) of our Lord and Savior Jesus Christ. Jesus said, "If anyone desires to be my disciple he must take up his cross and follow me" (Matt. 16:24-26). This is what identifies the crucified life: total self-denial and complete obedience to the Word of God. A crucifixion victim was forced to carry his cross to the execution site. This signified that his life was already over and destroyed his will to live. Thus the disciple "bears his cross," signifying death to the old nature and the loss of the will and desire to sin.

No one can live a crucified, holy life apart from total submission to God. As we submit ourselves to God, He will strengthen and empower us with the help of His Holy Spirit and enable us to submit to others. Apart from this relationship with God, our pride will dominate us and make it impossible for us to submit to anyone. But if we submit to the LORD, His strength will make us victorious in the crucified life (Phil 4:13). To pick up our cross and follow the Lord means to lose sight of our own personal desires and conform our lives to the example of Jesus Christ, even to the point of death (Phil. 2:5-8).

Meditate on These Scriptures

> I have been crucified with Christ (in Him I have shared His Crucifixion); it is no longer I who live, but Christ (the Messiah) lives in me; and the life I now live in the body I live by faith in (by adherence to and reliance on and complete trust in) the Son of God, Who loved me and gave Himself up for me. (Gal. 2:20 Amplified Bible)

> And who is he who will harm you if you are eager to do good? But even if you should suffer for what is right, you are blessed. "Do not fear what they fear; do not be frightened." But in your hearts set apart Christ as Lord. Always be prepared to give an answer to everyone who asks you to give the reason for the hope that you have. But do this with gentleness and respect, keeping a clear conscience, so that those who speak maliciously against your good behavior in Christ may be ashamed of their slander. It is better, if it is God's will, to suffer for doing good than for doing evil. (1 Pet. 3:13-17 NIV)

Commit to Memory

Philippians 1:21: ***For me, to live is Christ and to die is gain.*** **(NIV)**

Holiness And The Crucified Life
(Part 3)

Why is it so difficult for many of us to submit ourselves to the will and commands of God? The answer is far more complex than just a disobedient heart. It is more than just disobedience that causes such rebellion. The very nature of all mankind is contrary to the humble character of the Holy Spirit, who is responsible for transforming our nature to that of our Savior. We are all born in sin (Ps. 51:5), therefore our hearts are rebellious and wicked by nature (Jer. 17:9). Because of this condition, we must be born again (John 3:1-6). Until we are truly born again of the Spirit and transformed by the power of the living God, we will continue in rebellion.

No one possesses the power to change without the help of God. Only He can transform our lives with His Word and the indwelling of His Holy Spirit. Even after we have surrendered our lives to Jesus Christ, we must continue to constrain the nature of the flesh, which desires to have dominion over our actions and satisfy its desires. The key to this victory is steadfast prayer and Bible study. This is the only way to keep our minds on God and the things that are important to Him. If we continue steadfastly in prayer and Bible study, God will transform our minds and cause us to think as He thinks. We will have the mind of Christ (1 Cor. 2:11-16).

Although it may sound unrealistic, it is absolutely true. The Lord Jesus Christ is the Word of God made flesh (John 1:1); and if we make the Bible a regular part of our lives—studying its principles and applying them to our lives regularly—we will be one with the Lord. Once we reach this stage, we are walking in total holiness and exemplifying a life that is pleasing to God. This is what the apostle Paul described in Romans 12:2 as being transformed by renewing the mind. Constant reading and application of the Word of God is what renews the mind. Just as hearing the Word of God develops faith (Rom. 10:17), studying the Word transforms the mind.

The Bible is a powerful, life-changing source if we submit ourselves to God and allow it to be an integral part of our lives. This entire life-changing transformation takes place in the mind. However, there are some things that must happen in the process. The first step is to close the door on our past. We must remember that we are new creations in Christ and God does not condemn those who walk in holiness (Rom. 8:1,32-39). If we don't let go of our past, we won't walk in the future that God has designed specifically for our lives. No one can serve GOD while focusing on the things of the past (Luke 9:62). Take notice of these important points.

- We must put the past behind to reach the goal ahead (Phil. 3:13-15).
- Holding onto our past can be detrimental (Gen. 19:15-26).
- Continuing to dwell on our past misfortunes and hardships will sometimes cause us to blame or distrust God (2 Chron. 16:9). God neither tempts anyone nor can He Himself be tempted (James 1:13-14). Most of our mistakes and hardships are a result of bad choices we've made without first seeking God (Prov. 3:5-6).

- Our anxieties over things we have no control over will prevent us from living the crucified, holy life, but if we trust God we will have peace (Luke 12:22-31; Phil. 4:6-7).
- If you have an unforgiving heart, you cannot walk in holiness or receive the gift of salvation (Matt. 6:14-15).

A very important aspect of living the crucified, holy life is changing our way of thinking, or renewing our minds. The Bible says, "Do not be conformed to this world, but be ye transformed by the renewing of your mind" (Rom. 12:2a). To walk in the crucified life means to accept the life of a servant of God and of mankind. The only way we can accept this role is if we change our way of thinking. We must dispel our present way of thinking and view ourselves as servants of God and of all mankind. We must begin to think like our Savior Jesus Christ. The Lord taught His disciples that the first would be last and the last first (Mark 9:33-35) exemplifying humility and a submissive spirit.

Although He was equal with God, He came to this world to serve (Matt. 20:25-28). He displayed exemplary humility, obedience, faith, and character. Our Savior laid down His heavenly privileges and became a servant (Phil. 2:6-8). To sum up the crucified life, we must love the LORD God with all of our heart and love our neighbors as ourselves (Matt. 22:36-40). This exemplifies the crucified, holy life of an obedient servant of God.

Meditate on These Scriptures

> Therefore, since Christ suffered for us in the flesh, arm yourselves also with the same mind, for he who has suffered in the flesh has ceased from sin, that he no longer should live the rest of his time in the flesh

for the lust of men, but for the will of God. For we have spent enough of our past lifetime in doing the will of the Gentiles—when we walked in lewdness, lusts, drunkenness, revelries, drinking parties, and abominable idolatries. (1 Pet. 4:1-3 NKJV)

Dear friends, do not be surprised at the painful trial you are suffering, as though something strange were happening to you. But rejoice that you participate in the sufferings of Christ, so that you may be overjoyed when His glory is revealed. If you are insulted because of the name of Christ, you are blessed, for the Spirit of glory and of God rest on you. If you suffer, it should not be as a murderer or thief or any kind of criminal, or even as a meddler. However, if you suffer as a Christian, do not be ashamed, but praise God that you bear that name. For it is time for judgment to begin with the family of God; and if it begins with us, what will the outcome be for those who do not obey the gospel of God? And, "If it is hard for the righteous to be saved, what will become of the ungodly and the sinner?"

So then, those who suffer according to God's will should commit themselves to their faithful Creator and continue to do good. (1 Pet. 4:12-19 NIV)

Commit to Memory

Romans 12:2: ***And do not be conformed to this world, but be transformed by the renewing of your mind, that you may prove what is that good and acceptable and perfect will of God.*** **(NKJV)**

Holiness and the Crucified Life
(Part 4)

God the Father and the Lord Jesus Christ demand total reverence and praise. Living the crucified, holy life means understanding that God is Holy and that He (Jesus and God are one) must be praised and worshiped accordingly. We must always be mindful that God can neither look upon sin nor condone any form of sin that may reside in our hearts. Our heavenly Father is the perfect, sinless Creator of the universe, full of love, grace, and mercy. He is worthy of all our praise, worship, and reverence. The Bible clearly teaches the awesome Holiness of God and the importance of our praise and worship for him. We must reverence and praised Him.

The psalmist said it perfectly when he stated, "Let everything that has breath praise the LORD" (Ps. 150:6). Praise is an integral part of living a holy, crucified life. When we're living a holy, crucified life, praise will come naturally. The better we know the LORD, the more we will want to praise and worship Him. Our individual praise may not all look the same, but the principle of our praise and worship should be the same as that of the founders of the church of Jesus Christ (the disciples of the Lord). It should glorify God, lift up the name of Jesus Christ as Savior, and come directly from our hearts.

When we are truly living the holy, crucified life, we won't need anyone to tell us how to praise and worship God because our worship and praise for God will come naturally, regardless of our present circumstances. Walking in holiness means understanding that our worship and praise for God is not predicated on our present circumstances or the way we may feel at a particular time. Our praise and worship is based solely on who He is—the Almighty God. Take notice of the examples of worship offered to God the Father and our Savior Jesus Christ. These examples highlight the deity of both God the Father and the Son.

- God is sovereign, and every knee will bow to Him (Isa. 45:18-25).
- Every knee must bow and every tongue must confess He is Lord (Phil. 2:10-11).
- Even the heavenly hosts worship Him with awe (Rev. 5:11-14).

As we grow in the life of holiness, a number of things will begin to happen in our lives. The first thing we will notice is an increase in our faith. As we walk in holiness, which is obedience, God will answer many of our prayers because they will be in line with His will for our lives. As a result of God's actions, our faith will begin to skyrocket and our praise and worship will follow suit. Another important thing that will happen as we grow in holiness is significant growth in our ability to praise and worship the Creator in circumstances that we could not have in times past. Below are three good examples of worship and praise derived from walking in holiness.

- Daniel continued to pray even in the midst of serious peril (Dan. 6:6-10).
- The holy servants of God honored Him even when they were in danger of losing their lives (Dan. 3:15-18).
- After being warned of persecution, Paul still traveled to Jerusalem to spread the gospel of Jesus Christ (Acts 21:10-14).

Those who live the holy, crucified life understand God's promises. However, they are willing to accept the bad along with the good. They know that God loves us and will cause all things to work together for our good (Rom. 8:28). They should be our examples of walking in holiness.

- The crucified servant of God accepts and understands trials (James 1:2-3).
- He gives thanks for God's blessings even in his own trials (Job 1:20-22).
- Paul learned to give thanks regardless of his situation (Phil. 4:10-13).

We should draw inner strength from examples of those who lived the crucified life and endured hardship and then received the reward from God for their obedience and steadfastness. These examples are intended to teach, guide, and instruct us in our daily walk with God.

- Joseph lived the crucified, holy life and endured suffering, and God rewarded him (Gen. 41:38-44).
- Job endured some of the most severe trials known to man, yet he continued to live the holy life pleasing to God and received the reward (Job 42:10-17).

- Jesus Christ exemplified total humility and obedience and God the Father placed His name above all names (Phil. 2:5-11).

The holy crucified life is a life of spiritual victory, but it is not necessarily a life of natural success, as many of us might view success (Heb. 11:35-40). God views a successful life as one that impacts the lives of others in ways that effect positive change and spiritual growth (Matt. 28:18-20). Man's views are quite different from God's; man views success by one's net worth and the number of accomplishments that he/she achieves here on earth. Let us begin to live the crucified, holy life by obeying God's commands regardless of how uncomfortable they may make us feel, being mindful that our obedience enables God to reward us according to His promises.

Meditate on These Scriptures

> Therefore gird up the loins of your mind, be sober, and rest your hope fully upon the grace that is to be brought to you at the revelation of Jesus Christ; as obedient children, not conforming yourselves to the former lusts, as in your ignorance; but as He who called you is holy, you also be holy in all your conduct, because it is written, "Be holy, for I am holy." (1 Pet. 1:13-16 NKJV)

> But whatever was to my profit I now consider loss for the sake of Christ. What is more, I consider everything a loss compared to the surpassing greatness of knowing Christ Jesus my Lord, for whose sake I have lost all things. I consider them rubbish, that I may gain Christ and be found in Him, not having a righteousness of my own that comes from the law, but

that which is through faith in Christ—the righteousness that comes from God and is by faith. I want to know Christ and the power of His resurrection and the fellowship of sharing in His sufferings, becoming like Him in His death, and so, somehow, to attain to the resurrection from the dead. (Phil. 3:7-11 NIV)

Commit to Memory

Matthew 7:12: ***So in everything, do to others what you would have them do to you, for this sums up the law and the prophets.*** **(NIV)**

21

The Devil's Deception

To live the life God has purposed for us we must always be mindful of the adversary and his wicked schemes. Many of us fail to reach our full potential because we allow the adversary (Satan) to interfere with God's plans for our lives (he can only do what God allows [Job 1:1-12]). Often those of us who believe that we are spiritually mature and seasoned are the first to be deceived by the adversary's schemes. His most effective tools are deception, temptation, and distraction. As simple as it may seem, these tools have been effective for centuries.

In the very beginning, the devil (in the form of the serpent) deceived Eve. Adam followed his wife, and as a result mankind was spiritually separated from God (Gen. 3:1-8). Satan also knew Solomon's weakness and tempted him, causing him to disobey God and serve many false gods (1 Kings 11:1-13). However, his greatest claim to fame may be keeping the lost from seeing the light of the gospel (2 Cor. 4:4). In the wilderness the devil even tried to tempt the Lord, who had fasted for forty days, by using his typical weapons that include pride, things, and prestige (Matt. 4:1-11). However, God cannot be tempted.

The devil and his cohorts (Rev. 12:3-4; many believe that the third of the stars represent fallen angels, who along with Satan rebelled against God) usually attempt to lead us into a false sense of fulfillment and contentment. This lie is designed to cause us to believe that we are already doing plenty enough in terms of ministry. If he can keep us in this state, we will never reach the plans God has prepared for us (Eph. 2:10). The devil loves complacent, compromising Christians because they are no threat to his kingdom. If we are lackadaisical and consistently compromising sound Christian views in order to please others (even other Christians), then we are lukewarm Christians (Rev. 3:14-22).

We must stay alert and focused on our purpose and calling, keeping our minds on the LORD and crucifying our flesh daily by refusing to submit to anything that is contrary to sound doctrine. The devil wants to make us believe that living a holy life is boring and that we are missing out on something. However, the truth of the matter is, nothing is more exciting than serving the living God. The Christian life is exciting because we never know what God is going to do next in our lives. Often times the feeling we get that something is missing is the Spirit of God trying to draw us into a closer relationship with Him.

Accepting the nudging of the Holy Spirit and entering into a close relationship with God is the best weapon for learning to recognize the devil's deceptions. The closer we are to God, the more discerning we will become of evil and the devil's deceptive schemes (John 16:13-15). The Holy Spirit will tell us what is from God and what isn't. He doesn't speak to us audibly, but if we are walking upright with God we will be able to hear the Holy Spirit speaking to our hearts and warning us of present dangers (John 14:26). Often the Spirit speaks to us, and we choose to lean on our own understanding and do otherwise; this grieves the Spirit.

We are wise if we take heed to the principles of the Bible and listen to the voice of God speaking to our hearts and guiding us in the right direction. Only the Spirit of God can alert us and keep us from falling into the devil's deceptive schemes. The Holy Spirit is our Helper, Comforter, and Strengthener. He is the Spirit of God living inside of every Christian, revealing the truth and enlightening our minds so that we can understand the meaning of God's Word and His plans for our future. The Spirit is the promise from God to all believers (Luke 24:44-49; Acts 2:29-35; Eph. 1:3-14).

The devil will use any means possible to get God's children to carry out his wicked schemes. His primary motive in this is to disrupt God 's plans for us. He used King David to stir God's anger against Israel (1 Chron. 21:1-7), and he used Peter in an attempt to stop God's plan of salvation (Matt. 16:21-23). Regardless of how difficult it is to believe, the adversary uses Christians on a regular basis in church services around the world. Because his ultimate plan is to silence or block the gospel from being heard, he will place demons in the church to distract us from hearing the gospel.

Satan will use anyone or anything at his disposal to distract and prevent us from receiving the message (Acts 16:16-24; 1 Thess. 2:17-18). These schemes are not new. The devil has been using the same methods from the beginning to carry out his wicked plans. However, if we are in tune (having our minds consistently on the things of God and not the world) with the Spirit, we will not be deceived, for the Spirit will reveal to us what is from God and what is not.

The devil is a very formidable foe, but he can't launch his attacks against a Christian without God's permission (Job 1:6-12). He is a created being—created by God Almighty and by no means an equal or even a challenge for the God of the universe or His Son, Jesus Christ. So how can we contend with Satan? We can't, but the Holy Spirit, whom God has given to us, can (1 John 4:4). Notice that at the beginning of the thousand-year reign of Christ and the saints, God sends only one mighty angel to bind Satan and cast him into the bottomless pit (Rev. 20:1-3). God alone is omnipotent! This is what we must do to defeat our foe.

1. We must resist his delicacies (James 4:7).
2. We must be watchful and alert (1 Pet. 5:8-9; he wants us to believe only we're suffer).
3. Put on our armor daily (Eph. 6:12-18).
4. We must live a life of holiness (Gal 5:16-26).
5. Last but not least, we must pray for the faith to believe all that God has said and promised to those who confess and believe.

The devil is already defeated! Jesus Christ and all the saints of God are victorious. They have already received the victory over the devil and death at Calvary (1 Cor. 15:54-58). If we have confessed that Jesus Christ is Lord and truly believed in our hearts that God raised Him from the dead, we will not be fooled by the devil's deceptions.

Meditate on These Scriptures

> Be self-controlled and alert. Your enemy the devil prowls around like a roaring lion looking for someone to devour. Resist him, standing firm in the faith, because you know that your brothers throughout the world are undergoing the same kind of sufferings. And the God of all grace, who called you to His eternal glory in Christ, after you have suffered a little while, will Himself restore you and make you strong, firm and steadfast. To Him be the power forever and ever. Amen. (1 Pet. 5:8-11 NIV)

Now by this we know that we know Him, if we keep His commandments. He who says, "I know Him," and does not keep His commandments, is a liar, and the truth is not in him. But whoever keeps His word, truly the love of God is perfected in him. By this we know that we are in Him. He who says he abides in Him ought himself also to walk just as He walked. (1 John 2:3-6 NKJV)

Commit to Memory

1 Peter 5:9: ***Resist him, standing firm in the faith, because you know that your brothers throughout the world are undergoing the same kind of sufferings.*** **(NIV)**

22

Have the Cares of the World Caused You to Fall Away from God?

One of the greatest weapons the adversary has in his arsenal is the ability to divert us from our commitment and service to God. He will use any means possible to distract us and keep us occupied so that the time we spend alone with God is vastly limited and our service in ministry is anything but committed. His ultimate goal is to prevent us from establishing an intimate relationship with our Creator. He will often use the things of this present world to entice us and cause us to lust after worldly goods. He has this ability because he is the god of this present world system (2 Cor. 4:1-4).

The devil also used the same scheme when he tried to tempt Jesus in the wilderness after He had fasted for forty days and forty nights (Matt.4:1-11). The temptation of Jesus makes it crystal clear that Satan has authority over things and kingdoms. He certainly could not have offered them to the Lord if they were not in his possession. The devil knows that most of us like things, so he will use things in his attempts to distract and corrupt us by causing us to lust after things and ultimately become covetous and even envious of others because of the things they possess.

This is an extremely dangerous position for any of us to be in because it gives the devil power over that specific area of our life. If he controls any area of our life (emotions, finances, etc.), we will become distracted by the cares of this present world. Our thoughts will be dominated with what kind of car we drive, what type of house we live in, what type of clothes we wear, and how much money we have or don't have. Once we begin to live in this state, it will be easy for him to snatch God's message from us (Mark 4). Most of the devil's success comes from our inability to control the flesh.

The devil knows the more time we spend with God (praying, meditating on Scripture, and reading and studying the Bible), the less influence the things of this world will have on us and the more influence the Spirit of God will have on us. We will eventually adopt the mind of Christ if we persist steadfastly in the things of God. However, if we allow the adversary to keep us busy and distracted by the things of this world, we will never experience true closeness with God and will not be able to operate in the fullness of the power that's available to us through Christ. This is what the devil knows that many of us don't know:

1. He knows once we establish a relationship with God his influence on us will be weakened considerably (John 8:31-32; Rom. 6:16-18; Gal. 5:16).
2. A close relationship with the Lord will enable us to recognize the agents of the devil and their schemes (2 Cor. 11:12-15; 1 John 4:1).
3. Our adversary also knows that God will always reveal His ways to those who have an intimate relationship with Him (Ps. 37:23,24; 103:7).

Because the Word of God is the example that we must live by; we are to use it for instructions regarding our Christian walk. It is not mere words on paper or a collection of exciting stories. The Word of God is a wonderful, Spirit-filled arrangement of biblical history, prophecy, and poetry.

The Word of God is powerful and alive. There is no publication quite like it in the entire world. It is truly God's inspired Word poured out into the hearts of His prophets for the protection, edification, teaching, comforting, encouraging, guidance, counseling, and spiritual development of all mankind (1 Cor. 10:6; 2 Tim. 3:16-17). The Bible also equips those who read, study, and obey it with the ability to discern the intentions of one's heart (Heb. 4:12). It is imperative that we focus on spiritual things (the principles of Scripture) and not the things of this world (material). Keeping our minds on spiritual things will prevent us from being drawn away from God by the things of this world.

Allowing the cares of this world (things of material concern—cars, clothing, etc.) to dominate our thought process will cause us to become distracted from our commitment and service to God. It will eventually lead us down a path of disobedience and ultimately destroy our testimony. It can even cause the untimely destruction of our lives. This is usually the result of a lack of self-control and the strong desire to satisfy the cravings of the flesh. The only antidote is a steady dose of the Word of God mixed with prayer. It is also very important that we surround ourselves with those who are like-minded, for iron sharpens iron (Prov. 27:17).

The dangers of focusing on the cares of this world are very clear and apparent throughout the entire Bible. Here are some important examples.

1. Because Eli the priest allowed his love for his two sons to overshadow his responsibility to properly discipline them, it brought the judgment of God upon

his entire household and his seed for generations to come (1 Sam. 2:22-36; 4:19-22).

2. King Solomon in all his wisdom and knowledge could not control the overwhelming desires of his flesh, and as a result of this failure he began to worship false gods, ultimately destroying his relationship with the God of his father David (1 Kings 11:1-14).
3. Distraction caused the death of God's servant (1 Kings 13:1-32).
4. Greed and pride caused the death of two saints (Acts 5:1-11).

These examples were given to us from God to prevent us from failing in the same areas of our lives. We must always be mindful that God is a jealous God (Josh. 24:19-20), and He will not allow us to put anything or anyone before Him. God must always be first in our lives. Regardless of how much we love our mates and our children, God must come first (Luke 14:25-33). Anything that we put before God is an idol (TV, work, friends, and even family). God doesn't want us to hate our family; He simply wants us to love Him as He loves us. He loves us so much that He became a man and suffered crucifixion on the cross at Calvary to pay the debt in full for our sins so that we could be united with Him as He intended in the beginning.

1. First commandment: "You shall have no other gods before Me" (Deut. 5:7).
2. A follower of Jesus loves Him and keeps His word (John 14:23,24).
3. Jesus considers those who do God's will His family (Matt. 12:47-50).

Have you broken the Lord's heart? Is He still your first love; or have you found another? Return to your first love, honor Him, and He will honor you.

1. A love lost (Rev. 2:1-7).
2. Serve and honor God, and He will honor you (1 Sam. 2:29-30).

Meditate on These Scriptures

I speak in human terms because of the weakness of your flesh. For just as you presented your members as slaves of uncleanness, and of lawlessness leading to more lawlessness, so now present your members as slaves of righteousness for holiness. For when you were slaves of sin, you were free in regard to righteousness. What fruit did you have then in the things of which you are now ashamed? For the end of those things is death. But now having been set free from sin, and having become slaves of God, you have your fruit to holiness, and the end, everlasting life. For the wages of sin is death, but the gift of God is eternal life in Christ Jesus our lord. (Rom. 6:19-23 NKJV)

Now godliness with contentment is great gain. For we brought nothing into this world, and it is certain we can carry nothing out. And having food and clothing, with these we shall be content. But those who desire to be rich fall into temptation and a snare, and into many foolish and harmful lusts which drown men in destruction and perdition. For the love of money is a root of all kinds of evil, for which some have strayed from the faith in their greediness, and pierced themselves through with many sorrows. (1 Tim. 6:6-10 NKJV)

Commit to Memory

Romans 6:16: ***Do you not know that to whom you present yourselves slaves to obey, you are that one's slave whom you obey, whether of sin leading to death, or of obedience leading to righteousness?*** **(NKJV)**

23

The Character of a Christian

Character is the distinguishing element that defines who we are. Our character reveals who and what we represent, whether it is God or this present world. Our character as Christians should mimic the one we represent. Simply put, our character should be like the character of our Lord and Savior Jesus Christ. To be Christian means to be Christlike. We may never be sinless, but as followers of Jesus Christ we should sin far less than we did prior to our Christian conversion (2 Cor. 5:17; Eph. 4:21-32). The transforming power of the Holy Spirit helps us to do that as we pray, study the Bible daily, and submit our lives totally to the will of our heavenly Father.

There are some things that must be present in our character if we are truly followers of the Lord (2 Cor. 6:11-18; 7:1). I believe these principles are neither debatable nor negotiable. They will not make us perfect, but if followed they will help transform our lives. God does not expect perfection from us; what He does demand is a life of total obedience. This is not by any means an easy task. Throughout our Christian walk distractions, temptations, trials, and various obstacles will be present and will make it very challenging for us to live a life of obedience that identifies with good Christian character.

Regardless of the challenges we encounter, God is faithful and He will not allow us to be overtaken or overwhelmed by our challenges (Ps. 55:22; 1 Cor. 10:13). He has already equipped us with all that we need to succeed in our Christian walk—including His Spirit (Luke 10:19; John 14:15-18). For this reason we should walk in confidence as we allow the LORD to develop our Christian character, knowing that no weapon formed against us will prosper. Take notice of this important list of principles that should shape our Christian character.

1. We must live a life of obedience to God (Phil 2:5-8).
2. We must be willing to forgive (Matt. 6:14-15; 18:21,22).
3. We must learn to love our enemies or at least not hate them (Matt 5:43-48).
4. We must learn to deny our flesh and its demands (Gal. 5:24-26; Col. 3:5-11).
5. We must monitor what we view (Ps. 101:3; Matt. 5:27-30).
6. We must be living examples of the Lord for the whole world to see (Matt. 5:13-16).
7. We must always put the Lord first (Luke 14:26-33).

None of these examples can be accomplished without the power of the indwelling Holy Spirit. We must first learn to submit to the Spirit of God by making the things of God (prayer and Bible study) the number one priority in our lives. To successfully follow these commands (Christian principles), we must draw strength from the Word of God. Attending church regularly (although important) is only one part of the process of building Christian character. We must read, study the Bible, and meditate on the Word of God on a daily basis if we truly desire to develop the character that is pleasing to God.

Here are some keys to building Christian character. By following these steps we will become sensitive to the will of God and ultimately become more like our Savior (this is God's ultimate goal for us—to be like His Son).

1. To live the obedient life, we must study the Word of God (2 Tim. 2:15).
2. To be able to forgive, we must remind ourselves that Christ died for us (John 3:16).
3. To love our enemies, we must keep in mind that Christ died for us while we were still sinners (Rom. 5:6-8).
4. To deny our flesh, we must follow the example of Jesus Christ (Matt. 4:1-11).
5. We must make a covenant with our eyes and our mind (Job 31:1).

Of all the commands, gifts, and power, the greatest is love. The Lord sums it up like this; "'You shall love the LORD your God with all your heart, with all your soul, and with all your mind.' This is the first and great commandment. And the second is like it: 'You shall love your neighbor as yourself.' On these two commandments hang all the Law and the Prophets" (Matt. 22:37-40 NKJV). It is important that we notice that the second great (or greatest) commandment is to love your neighbor as yourself. Our character should always display love toward others (even those who are lost). Often our genuine love toward those who are not saved will draw them to Christ.

If we can find enough love in our hearts only for those who love us, we are in serious need of spiritual growth. Loving our friends and family is easy, but the true sign of good Christian character is the ability to love everyone. Jesus pointed out the importance of this love in the beatitudes (Matt. 5:43-48). Loving difficult people isn't easy, but it is necessary, and it is a clear indication of whether we are still dominated by the old sin nature or we are led by the Spirit and living in obedience to God. The way we treat others is so important because we are always being observed by others to see whether we truly walk the walk.

Our actions will determine what others think about Christianity and even Jesus Christ. For this reason it is very important that we make sure not to allow our emotions to erupt at every offense that may be fired at us. It is also very important to note that God is far more interested in our reaction to an offense than the offense itself. James (Jesus' brother) said to be quick to listen, slow to speak, and slow to anger (James 1:19). Without these qualities we will never be able to exemplify good Christian character. We must to be less sensitive in our emotions, understanding that we are not battling against the individual.

Our battle is always spiritual and always in our own minds. The results may manifest outwardly, but the battle is waged in our minds. This is the reason we must keep our minds on spiritual thing—so that when the battle occurs we are aware of what is happening and thus will respond correctly. If we are not aware of this spiritual battle when it occurs, it will have devastating effects on our character (our response will be the same as those who do not know Christ). However, if we are living in obedience to God, we will not be dominated by our natural emotions and desires (Gal. 5:16) because God's grace will sustain us.

A character that exemplifies love and total selflessness should be the goal every Christian strives to achieve. This character was displayed throughout the life and death of our Lord and Savior Jesus Christ, who serves as a perfect model for all Christians. The Bible says, "Your attitude should be the same as that of Christ Jesus" (Phil. 2:5 NIV). It is almost impossible for anyone to completely model the life of our Lord, but we must learn to love one another. Our love toward others is the proof that we truly belong to the family of God (1 John 4:7-16). When we learn to humble ourselves and love others, we will have the character that pleases God.

The apostle Paul said that even if you give your body to be burned and have not love, you profit nothing (1 Cor. 13:2-3). Love is the key! No matter how difficult it may be, we must learn to love others because it is the Lord's command. Our love toward others is essentially love toward Jesus Christ because we display our love through His Spirit in obedience to His Word. Just as we love God because He first loved us (John 3:16), we can love others because He loved us while we were still in our sins (Rom. 5:8). How can we possibly say we love God and yet not have love for others—especially for the lost?

God created each of us in His own image (Gen. 1:27); therefore we sin against God if we don't love those whom He created. We must learn to love the brethren, as does the Lord. God is love, and if His Spirit lives in us and has dominion over our lives, the character we display will appear very much like that of Jesus Christ. If He truly abides in us, we should be walking in the light (1 John 2:3-11). We must pray daily that God will fill our hearts with His Spirit on a daily basis and enable us to love those whom we otherwise could not love.

Meditate on These Scriptures

> "You are the salt of the earth; but if the salt loses its flavor, how shall it be seasoned? It is then good for nothing but to be thrown out and trampled under foot by men. You are the light of the world. A city that is set on a hill cannot be hidden. Nor do they light a lamp and put it under a basket, but on a lampstand, and it gives light to all who are in the house. Let your light shine before men, that they may see

your good works and glorify your Father in heaven. (Matt. 5:13-16 NKJV)

Therefore if there is any consolation in Christ, if any comfort of love, if any fellowship of the Spirit, if any affection and mercy, fulfill my joy by being like minded, having the same love, being of one accord, of one mind. Let nothing be done through selfish ambition or conceit, but in lowliness of mind let each esteem others better than himself. Let each of you look out not only for his own interest, but also for the interest of others. (Phil. 2:1-4 NKJV)

Commit to Memory

Galatians 5:16: ***I say then: Walk in the Spirit, and you shall not fulfill the lust of the flesh.*** **(NKJV)**

24

The Holy Spirit

Parakletos (Greek) – "one who speaks in favor of, as an intercessor, advocate, or legal assistant" *(Nelson's Illustrated Dictionary of the Bible)*.

The Holy Spirit, also known as the *Parakletos*, is the third person of the Trinity (Father, Son, and Holy Spirit). It is through the Holy Spirit that God reveals Himself, empowers individuals, and teaches us about Himself. Although He is a Spirit, the Lord refers to Him in almost human terms (John 14:17-26; 15:26; 16:5-15). He is gentle and appeared as a dove (Matt. 3:13-17), and He has emotions because He can be grieved by our behavior (Eph. 4:29-32). The Holy Spirit is the nucleus in the life of every Christian.

I believe if we are to truly understand the awesome nature of the Holy Spirit of God, we must closely examine the dove. Because the Holy Spirit was described as descending on the Lord Jesus as a dove after the baptism, we must take a close look at the characteristics of a dove to understand why this correlation was made.

Doves are beautiful, white birds. They appear to express affection, stroking each other and "billing and cooing." They mate for life, sharing nesting and parenting duties. They are gentle birds that never resist attack or retaliate against their enemies. Even when her young are attacked, a dove will give only a pitiful call of distress. Because of its innocence and gentle nature, the dove is a common religious symbol. The Holy Spirit took the form of a dove at Jesus' baptism (Matt. 3:16; Mark 1:10; Luke 3:22). The dove also symbolizes peace, love, forgiveness, and the church *(Nelson's Illustrated Dictionary of the Bible)*. Now we can understand the correlation between the Holy Spirit and the dove.

There isn't anything or anyone more important to us than the Holy Spirit. He is responsible for the rebirth/new birth of all believers (John 3:3-6). His role in our lives is so important because He is responsible for everything from spiritual growth to the distribution of spiritual gifts. Every single aspect of our Christian walk depends on our submission to Him. We must allow Him to have complete dominion over our entire lives if we desire to live in obedience to God. This means whenever we feel Him telling us in our spirit that something isn't right, we must obey and not lean on our own natural understanding.

Often the Spirit will speak to our hearts in regard to something as simple as our reaction to an offense hurled at us by someone who may or may not be close to us. He will tell us not to respond negatively; however, in many cases we will allow our pride to override the voice of the Spirit and respond in a manner that is totally contrary to the character of one who follows Jesus Christ. When we choose to disobey His voice, we grieve Him and place ourselves in a very dangerous spot. By choosing to make our own decisions, we are actually removing ourselves from underneath the umbrella of God's protection.

This does not mean that God no longer loves us or that we have lost our salvation. It simply means that our actions are telling God that we know what's best for us and we don't need His input.

It is like a king who chooses to travel without his royal bodyguards—he is on his own (and in harm's way). Until he decides to retrieve those who are appointed to protect him, he is without protection. God created each of us and knows exactly what is best for us; therefore, He gave us His Spirit to help us and protect us from making the wrong decisions. The work of the Holy Spirit is abundant in the life of all Christians. Here are some of the responsibilities the Bible lists for the Holy Spirit.

1. The Holy Spirit is our Comforter (John 14:16).
2. The Holy Spirit is our Teacher (John 14:26).
3. The Holy Spirit is our Witness for the Lord (John 15:26).
4. The Holy Spirit is our Truth in the Lord (John 16:13).
5. The Holy Spirit is our Helper (Rom. 8:26).
6. The Holy Spirit is our Intercessor and Advocate (Rom. 8:27)—compare Jesus' intercession (Rom. 8:34).
7. The Holy Spirit is the distributor of spiritual gifts (1 Cor. 12:1-11).

The Holy Spirit's nature is the same, as that of God the Father because He is God's very own Spirit (1 Cor. 2:10-11). He is the third person of the Trinity, equal with both God the Father and God the Son; thus He operates in the same power as God the Father and God the Son. He is omnipresent because He dwells in every believer (1 Cor. 6:19); He is omniscient because He searches the deep things of God (1 Cor. 2:10-12), He is omnipotent because He exercises the power of God (Zech. 4:6-7), He is in one accord, bearing witness in heaven with the Father and the Son in heaven and on earth (1 John 5:7,8), and He took part in the creation (Gen. 1:2, 26).

The Holy Spirit is the power of God living in those who believe in His Son. He is God's gift to all believers (Acts 2:38,39) and the very source of God's mighty power. This power is essential in overcoming strongholds and all kinds of attacks the adversary will launch against the children of God. To be triumphant in our daily walk, we must learn of the Holy Spirit and begin to acknowledge Him in all that we do. We must always be mindful that regardless of how much we read and how much Scripture we can memorize, the Holy Spirit is the very source of power that lives in us. Apart from His abiding presence, we would be lost.

Just as the Lord instructed all of His disciples to wait for the promise of the Father to arrive (Acts 1:4-8), we also must learn to exercise patience and obedience by waiting on the direction and guidance of the Holy Spirit before we make decisions. Generally our problems are a result of our impatience and leaning on our own understanding, which lead to bad decision making and poor judgment that in many cases becomes devastating. This devastation can sometimes takes a long period of time to repair—maybe even a lifetime. Because He knows all things, we must learn to acknowledge Him first (Prov. 3:5-6).

Because the Spirit is gentle like a dove, He will not force us to obey His voice. He will convict our spirit only when we are in the wrong. However, if we continue in our own ways (this should not happen if we are truly in Christ; 1 John 3:4-9), we will grieve Him. God loves us so much that He sent His Son (God in the flesh) to die a horrible death in order to pay the penalty for sin in full, and then He chose to live in us (in the person of the Holy Spirit) to enable us to fulfill the requirements of a follower of Jesus Christ (we couldn't do it without His abiding presence). His awesome acts of love toward us are astounding and far beyond what we can truly comprehend.

We must be mindful that we can quench the Spirit (1 Thess. 5:19), so let us continually give thanks to God for His powerful acts of love toward us and His wonderful gift of the Holy Spirit. Now that we understand His important role in our lives, we must begin to acknowledge Him in all that we do. Begin to thank the Holy Spirit when He gives you revelation or brings back to your remembrance a Scripture you were trying to recall. We must meditate on the Word of God in a quiet, private place and allow the Holy Spirit to feed our souls. We must make a mental note to acknowledge God in all that we do on a daily basis so that His Spirit can direct our steps and guide our paths.

As we begin to submit to Him and acknowledge His presence, the love of God will fill our hearts and allow the Spirit to have dominion over our lives. Allowing Him to pilot our lives is the only path to safety and true fellowship with God. Hallelujah!

Meditate on These Scriptures

> "But now I go away to Him who sent Me, and none of you asks Me, 'Where are you going?' But because I have said these things to you, sorrow has filled your heart. Nevertheless I tell you the truth. It is to your advantage that I go away; for if I do not go away, the Helper will not come to you; but if I depart, I will send Him to you. And when He has come, He will convict the world of sin, and of righteousness, and of judgment: of sin because they do not believe in Me; of righteousness because I go to My Father and you see me no more; of judgment, because the ruler of this world is judged." (John 16:5-12 NKJV)

"Therefore I say to you, every sin and blasphemy will be forgiven men, but the blasphemy against the Holy Spirit will not be forgiven men. Anyone who speaks a word against the Son of Man, it will be forgiven him; but whoever speaks against the Holy Spirit, it will not be forgiven him, either in this age or in the age to come." (Matt. 12:31-32 NKJV)

Commit to Memory

Romans 8:16: ***The Spirit Himself bears witness with our spirit that we are children of God.*** **(NKJV)**

25

What's Wrong with the Church?

What's wrong with the church? Many of us would answer that question by saying, "Nothing." If that's our answer, then why isn't the church transforming lives today as it did in the early church? To answer that question we must go back to the beginning and examine the early church. In the early church, the awesome power and presence of the Holy Spirit empowered the followers of Jesus Christ (church founders) to carry out the work God called them to do through His Son. The Bible says about three thousand were saved when Peter preached the gospel (Acts 2:31-41), the apostles prayed for boldness and were filled with the Spirit (Acts 4:23-31), and the Spirit of God humbled the hearts of the early believers as they united with one accord, sharing their goods so that none were without (Acts 4:32-37).

So where is the power of the Holy Spirit today? I personally do not claim to have all the answers; however, I know if we study and obey the Word of God that we will find the answers to the majority of our questions (if we seek with all our heart, we will find [Jer. 29:13; Luke 11:9,10]). I believe it all starts with obedience to the Word of God—certainly in relation or regard to church development and leadership. We must follow the rules and blueprint in the Bible when establishing leadership and order in the church. The Bible is quite clear in regard to God's calling and choosing leaders in the service of the church.

God always called men to lead His people. God created Adam first and gave him dominion over all of the earth and allowed him to name all the animals. God chose Moses to lead Israel when He could have raised up a woman to lead His people. Of all the Old Testament and New Testament prophets (John the Baptist is considered by many to be the last Old Testament prophet), none of them were women. When the Lord chose His twelve apostles, He chose only men. God does use women in doing the work of His kingdom, but He always calls men to lead the people. Women are no lesser than men, however, this is simply the order in which God has chosen.

This does not mean that women shouldn't or can't prophesy and render service—of course they will, and they do. This simply means that from a position of leadership in the church God always has chosen men. God put the man in a deep sleep and created a woman from one of his ribs and then allowed the man to name her (he named her woman because she came from man). The woman was created to be the man's helper and not his leader, pastor, teacher, or bishop (Gen. 2:18-24; 1 Cor. 11:7-12). God does not permit a woman to have authority over a man (1 Tim. 2:12-15). Many of us struggle with the preceding Scripture and attempt to ascribe it to the apostle Paul's personal opinion. If we believe that this particular Scripture is only from Paul, then we will be forced to abandon 2 Timothy 3:16!

In many of our churches, women are usurping authority over men. Women are preaching, teaching men, leading men's ministries, and leading entire assemblies. Our pastors and church leaders are placing women in offices that God has not ordained them to be in. Just because an office is vacant doesn't mean that just anyone available should fill the void. We must obey the Word of God (1 Sam. 15:17-26). This by no means is an attempt to discredit or diminish the importance of women.

I personally believe that without the presence of women this world would look much like a desert—because men would destroy each other. God loves women the same as He does men, but according to the teaching of the Bible, God has a desired order, placing the man in headship over the woman. I know that God uses women as well as men to advance the gospel because it's in the Bible (Joel 2:28-30 fulfilled on Pentecost; Acts 2:12-21), and I have seen it in my own life. Women are just as important to the growth of the church and the advancement of the gospel as men. Unfortunately, many are not satisfied unless they are the head of the assembly.

The truth of the matter is God loves each of us and considers each of us to be very important, regardless whether or not we lead the assembly. We can't all be bishops, pastors, or deacons, but we can all be obedient to the Word of God and allow Him to direct us where He desires us to be. We are all a part of the body of Christ, with each of us having our own specific function to carry out to the best of our ability. The husband who provides spiritually, emotionally, and financially for his family and the wife who, being filled with the Spirit of God, supports her husband and raises up her children in the admonition of the LORD are no less important than the preacher who ministers to the assembly every Sunday.

God is not like us; He shows no favoritism toward anyone (Acts 10:34-38; Rom. 2:11) but accepts all who are obedient to His Word. Somehow we have to allow God to break the pride inside of us that causes us to believe that it is more important to lead (even when we haven't been called or chosen) than to be obedient or to receive promotion from man than placement from God. We must realize that God will not reward us according to our titles or rank. God is not concerned with any of that because He judges the heart (1 Sam. 16:4-7). Regardless of what your title is or how you portray yourself to people, God knows your heart and your intentions. He desires obedience above all else.

We must repent of any lack of obedience to the order God has established for all of mankind. In order for the Spirit of God to move in our service, we must pay close attention to the requirements the apostle Paul gave Timothy regarding bishops, deacons (1 Tim. 3:1-13), and elders (Titus 1:5-9). It is very important for Christians understand Paul was led by the Spirit of God and not just giving his personal opinions when writing the scriptures (2 Pet. 1:19-21). I don't believe it is by any means a small thing or an oversight that Paul stated these offices should be filled by husbands of one wife (meaning men).

Many believe this issue is no big deal and simply harmless, but disobedience is a sin regardless of whether it is a result of ignorance or not. The Bible does not leave it to us to decide whether we have to obey or not, and it makes it clear and easy for us to understand what God desires of us with examples of people just like us. The prophet Samuel told Saul that obedience is better than sacrifice and disobedience is as witchcraft (1 Sam. 15:22,23). Consequently, Saul's disobedience caused him to lose the kingdom to David. Why is it so important that our leaders are chosen and appointed by God?

1. The anointing flows from the leader (Ps. 133:1-3).
2. A rotten leader will affect an entire congregation (1 Cor. 5:6-8).
3. Man chooses according to availability and or appearance; God chooses according to the heart of a man (1 Sam. 16:7-12).

God requires full obedience from all of His children. And those of us who are in positions of leadership bear a greater responsibility in this. The absence of leadership by men not only has affected the church but also has crept into our homes and our communities. Today women lead more than sixty-five percent of all households across this country. As a result of man's inability to stand in headship, young men and women are suffering the consequences. As leaders of the church, we (men) must return to God's commands; and as fathers and examples for young men and women, we must take the role of headship that God has appointed to us.

1. The head of woman is man, and the head of man is Christ (1 Cor. 11:1-3).
2. The man is the head of the household (Eph. 5:22-33).
3. The husband must honor his wife, or he will not be able to communicate with God through prayer (1 Pet. 3:7).

This is by no means an attempt to diminish God's role for women in ministry. Women are extremely important in the eyes of God in ministry, the world in general, and in the home. However, the Bible is clear on the subject of leadership in the church and headship in the home. This is no knock on women but a message to all men who claim to be of God. As men we have the greater responsibility. We are to provide for our families financially and emotionally and to be the spiritual leaders for our households (Col. 3:19,21; Prov. 22:6). This is our first and most important ministry. God expects us to place our family before everything except Him. Those who don't properly provide for their own families are not of God (1 Tim. 5:8).

Regardless of the title(s) we hold in church or the ministry we lead, our own families should always take precedence. Many of our ministries are not being empowered by the Holy

Spirit because those who are leading them are not in control of their own homes. The Bible is crystal clear in regard to the church leaders having full control of their own homes prior to taking leadership in the church (1 Tim. 3:1-13). God is fully aware of the importance of learning to lead a few before we can lead many. Often God will prepare us for leadership when we are not even aware of it. He prepared King David while he was herding sheep (1 Sam. 16:1-13).

It is very important that we take this matter of disobedience to God's required order for church leadership very seriously if we desire to see the power of God working in our midst. If we don't begin to follow the commands of Scripture regarding the operation of the body of Christ (the church), we will begin to regress. In fact, I believe our regression has already begun. Look at the condition of the church today, and it seems we strike an eerie resemblance to the world. Our divorce rate is almost identical to that of the world, many of our church leaders dress and carry themselves in the same fashion as the world, and God's house has become more of a business than a ministry.

Many of our so-called Christian performers mimic the performances of those in the secular world (sometimes you can't tell one from the other). God has gifted His church with so many talents and gifts, yet many of us have put our hands to the plow and can't stop looking backwards. The Lord said those of us who fashion our lives this way are not fit for service in his kingdom (Luke 9:62). We can't possibly be the salt and light that the Lord said we should be if we look and act just like the world (unsaved). Why can't we just do what the Bible teaches us to do? We don't need special programs or well-organized group fasts—just obedience.

God isn't worried about rewriting Scripture to reach the postmodern generation, the baby boomers, X generation, homosexuals, lesbians, or any other so-called special interest group or organization. The canon is complete; Jesus Christ is the same yesterday, today, and forever (Heb. 13:8). God's grace is sufficient for all of mankind, and we place ourselves in a very dangerous and compromising position when we make any attempt to change the message that the Lord died for our sins and that God raised Him from the dead, enabling those who believe in their hearts and confess with their mouths that He is Lord to receive the gift of eternal life.

The Bible says that to the unbeliever this message is foolishness because they lack spiritual discernment—they are unable to understand spiritual things (1 Cor. 2:12-14). Are we any more spiritually discerning that they are if we believe that we have to change the message to reach those who are perishing? Is God Omniscient? Of course He is! He certainly knew from the beginning exactly to whom we would have to minister the gospel today. God's plan of redemption is perfect because He is the creator of all things and knows the beginning and the end of all things. Nothing that we experience is a surprise to God nor is it uncommon to Him because he knows each and every one of us personally.

The same gospel that the apostle Peter used to reach three thousand souls two thousand years ago (Acts 2) will do the same today if the messengers are preaching the gospel undiluted, living in obedience to God, not focused on pleasing people, and living lives out loud that are sold out for Jesus Christ. Anything less will only render the same type of results that we have grown accustomed to (all emotions and no true power). The same power that worked in the early church, producing signs and wonders, is still available through the same Spirit who lives in God's people today. We simply have to do what the Bible says without making modifications.

It is paramount that we understand that Paul's letters to Timothy were specifically for the structure, development, and order of the body of Christ, the church (1 Tim. 3:14-16). This is why it is so important that we follow the guidelines therein. These letters (1 and 2 Timothy and Titus—the

Pastoral Epistles) are basically blueprints for church formation and were instrumental to Timothy and Titus then, and they should be instrumental to us today also. There is no need to make adjustments or changes to anything that is written in these epistles in order to suit or fit any particular situation because God's Word is relevant to all and for all situations.

I pray that the church will return to full obedience to the Word of God so that His awesome Spirit can work in and through us as God intended. Certainly God knows the plans He has for us. That is why He gave us His spirit—because He knew we could not be successful without Him. The work that is required for us today is no less challenging than it was for our church founders, and God does not require any less from us than He did from them. That is why He has given us His Holy Spirit. So let us all return to God in total obedience so that we can be fully equipped with His power to do His will. If we honor Him He will honor us.

The church will not experience the awesome power of the Holy Spirit that was present in the early church until we return to full obedience to God's Word.

Meditate on These Scriptures

> So Samuel said: "Has the LORD as great delight in burnt offerings and sacrifices, as in obeying the voice of the LORD? Behold, to obey is better than sacrifice, and to heed than the fat of rams. For rebellion is as the sin of witchcraft, and stubbornness is as iniquity and idolatry. Because you have rejected the word of the LORD, He has also rejected you from being King." (1 Sam. 15:22-23 NKJV)

> Remember those who rule over you, who have spoken the word of God to you, whose faith follow, considering the outcome of their conduct. Jesus Christ is

the same yesterday, today, and forever. Do not be carried about with various and strange doctrines. For it is good that the heart be established by grace, not with foods which have not profited those who have been occupied with them. (Heb. 13:7-9 NKJV)

Commit to Memory

2 Timothy 3:16-17: ***All scripture is given by inspiration of God, and is profitable for doctrine, for reproof, for correction, for instruction in righteousness, that the man of God may be complete, thoroughly equipped for every good work.*** **(NKJV)**

26

The Thief Comes to Steal

Jesus said, "The thief does not come except to steal, and to kill, and to destroy. I have come that they may have life, and that they may have it more abundantly" (John 10:10 NKJV). Jesus addresses Satan as the thief because his primary mission is stealing the truth from unbelievers so they don't believe, and from believers so they'll be less effective in ministry (service to the lost and the church). The devil hasn't changed since the beginning (John 8:44). He still uses the same schemes and devices—deception, enticement, and distraction to steal the truth (God's Word—John 17:17; Mark 4:14-15) from both unbelievers and believers.

- Satan's clever scheme deceived Eve (Gen. 3:2-8; cf. Gen. 2:16-17).
- Satan used lust to bring sin on the house of David (2 Samuel 11-13).
- The devil uses our own flesh to hinder us by causing us to focus so much on the messenger that we are not able to receive the message (Mark 6:2-5).

The devil is usually very subtle with his spiritual attacks. He will use everything at his disposal to steal all of our hopes and our faith. Take notice of all the things that begin to happen when you attempt to listen to the preached Word, study the Word of God, pray, or meditate on the gospel. Although he is spirit, he will use natural things to distract you. The phone may ring, you may get hungry, someone may knock at your door, you may become very sleepy, you might remember there was something you were supposed to do, or someone may scream in church and distract you from hearing the intended message. None of these things are coincidences.

Satan attacks each of us according to our level of spiritual development. He will not use the same methods on the saved that he uses on the unsaved, and he will not use the same methods on those of us who study the Bible daily as he uses on those who just attend church on Sunday. What many of us just don't understand is that when we came into this world we belonged to the enemy because we are born into sin (Ps. 51:5). For this very reason every one of us must be born again (John 3:1-7). This may at first seem complicated, but it is really simple once you understand how it all started.

The devil (in the form of a serpent) deceived Eve while she and Adam were in the garden. Adam disobeyed God's command by following his wife and eating from the tree of the knowledge of good and evil, which God forbade him to do (Gen. 2:16-17). This act of disobedience severed his previous close union with God and also forfeited his title deed to the world (Gen. 1:27-28; 2:19) to Satan. Many may dispute this statement, but we do know that the devil tried to tempt Jesus in the desert by offering Him the kingdom, and he couldn't offer it unless it was in his control (Matt. 4:1-11).

There is no question that God has complete dominion over the entire earth (Ps.24:1-2); however, there also should be no dispute regarding the devil's authority because the Bible points out that Satan is the god of this present world system (2 Cor. 4:4). The Bible also says that the whole world is under his power (1 John 5:19).

Some of us want to reject these kinds of statements because we tend to think that anyone who is controlled by the enemy (or has a demon living inside) would spend most of his/her time committing murders or some other heinous crimes. The fact is that anyone who does not have the Spirit of God living inside of him/her has the spirit of the world in His place. No human being has complete, autonomous control of himself/herself. Take, for example, the parable that the Lord told regarding the man who had an evil spirit (Matt. 12:43-45). Also notice that everyone from whom the Lord cast demonic spirits received Him afterwards.

When we receive salvation through Jesus Christ, we welcome in the presence of the Holy Spirit (God's gift to all believers), who makes His home in us. His presence prevents any demons from entering us or taking any sort of control of our actions. Contrary to that old saying, "The devil made me do it," when Christians fall, it's simply a matter of a lack of self-control. If a righteous man/woman falls they will rise and be redeemed (Prov. 24:16). We will never be overtaken by our mistakes–if we repent. So when we fall, we must resist the enemy's attempts to make us feel guilty to the point of self-condemnation.

This is another tool that the devil will use to steal our freedom in Christ. If he can make us feel like we've committed such an atrocity that we cannot be forgiven, then he has defeated us. This lie is totally contrary to the Bible and does not at all resemble the loving and forgiving nature of God. Jesus paid our debt in full, and we don't have to do anything except walk in obedience to the Word of God. The Bible says if we confess, we will be forgiven (1 John 1:9); and if we are walking after the Spirit, we will not be condemned (Rom.

8:1-6). So how is it that we allow ourselves to be deceived by the enemy? The answer is simple: we are focusing on him and this present world system and not on God.

If we focus on God and the things of God, then the enemy becomes powerless. It is extremely important that we understand that he can't take anything from us that we don't allow him to have. If we are children of God, then he must approach God prior to attempting to take anything from us or even attacking us (Job 1:6-12). If we know the Word of God, we can use it to quench all of his fiery darts and wicked temptations because the Bible functions as a shield and a sword. It will protect us from his attacks if we use it, and it becomes an offensive weapon as we pray and speak it. It is imperative that we know how to prevent the devil from stealing from us.

Jesus promised us that the Holy Spirit would bring the Word of God back to our remembrance when in need (John 14:26); however, He can only bring back what we put in. If we're not studying the Word of God on a daily basis, it can't be brought back because it's not there to bring back. If we're not on post (focused), Satan will steal everything that God has for us (1 Pet. 5:8-9). As difficult as it may seem, God has and will continue to allow the devil to launch various trials against us. God allows this so that we can grow and mature spiritually. It is the only way that we will develop the necessary experience to make an impact on the world. Our trials will also equip us to help others, who will experience the same struggles.

What's important for us to know is we will all suffer persecution and trials (2 Tim. 3:12) from those who oppose the gospel; however, God will never allow us to suffer or be tempted beyond what we can stand (1 Cor. 10:13) because He can identify with our pain. Although He is God, Jesus Christ became like us and suffered while also being tempted (Heb. 2:18). He understands all of our experiences—even the devil's attempts to deceive us and steal everything from us that God has provided. Our heavenly Father has provided us with everything we need to prevent the enemy from stealing what belongs to us or deceiving us.

The devil is a defeated foe. He is by no means to be taken lightly or totally disregarded, but no Christian should fear him. We all must get serious about our Christian walk, knowing that we have an enemy who is doing all that he possibly can to deceive us and steal what God has provided for us. The devil is using every resource at his disposal to succeed in his wicked, crafty schemes. If we know that he is using everything at his disposal to destroy us, why aren't we using what was given to us to protect ourselves? If we're using the Word of God, then what we have is safe.

If we're not using the principles of Scripture, then what we have is at risk. Only the Word of God has the power to stop the enemy in his tracks and prevent him from stealing what belongs to us and destroying our testimony. If we are reading and studying the Bible daily and living in obedience to God, then we will experience the abundant life our Lord and Savior Jesus Christ has promised us.

Meditate on These Scriptures

> But what I do, I will also continue to do, that I may cut off the opportunity of those who desire an opportunity to be regarded just as we are in the things of which they boast. For such are false apostles, deceitful workers, transforming themselves into apostles of Christ. And no wonder! For Satan himself transforms himself into an angel of light. Therefore it is no great thing if his ministers also transform themselves into ministers of righteousness, whose end will be according to their works. (2 Cor. 11:12-15 NKJV)

Then the LORD said to Satan, "Have you considered my servant Job, that there is none like him on the earth, a blameless and upright man, one who fears God and shuns evil? And still he holds fast to his integrity, although you incited Me against him, to destroy him without cause." So Satan answered the LORD and said, "Skin for skin! Yes, all that a man has he will give for his life. But stretch out your hand now, and touch his bone and his flesh, and he will surely curse You to Your face!" And the LORD said to Satan, "Behold he is in your hand, but spare his life." So Satan went out from the presence of the LORD, and struck Job with painful boils from the sole of his foot to the crown of his head. (Job 2:3-7 NKJV)

Commit to Memory

2 Corinthians 11:14: ***And no wonder, for Satan himself masquerades as an angel of light.*** **(NIV)**

27

Under Pressure

The term "under pressure" can be described as being in a severe or intense state of distress or experiencing a period of extreme anguish. From a Christian perspective, being under pressure is usually defined as going through a trial. Often we relate our trials and struggles to Satan, but if we study Scripture closely, we will find that all trials ultimately come from God (Job 1:1-12). The devil is the accuser and the inflictor, but God ultimately has the last say. This means that to credit Satan for our trials is immature, ignorant, and dishonoring to God. Trials are not designed to destroy us or keep us under pressure but are intended to develop us, equip us to help and comfort others, and draw us closer to God.

- Trials develop our patience and faith (James 1:2-4).
- Trials will strengthen and perfect us (1 Pet. 5:8-10)
- Our trials will also lead us to glorify God (Dan. 4:24-37).

All Christians at some point will be placed under the intense pressure of some sort of trial. What's important for each of us to understand is how to react under this intense pressure. There is no ironclad formula designed by anyone (certainly not by me) to prepare ourselves for the trials that we know are eventually going to come. However, because all trials are ultimately from God we must learn to follow the proper examples in Scripture to weather these storms and please God while we are learning what it is that He intends for us to learn from these experiences. Here is a list of some important principles that will assist us while we are under the intense pressure of a trial.

1. Regardless of how severe it seems, always trust God (Dan 3:14-28).
2. Encourage yourself in the LORD (1 Sam. 30:6-8).
3. Don't murmur and complain about the situation (Phil. 2:14-15).
4. Always praise God in every situation so that your example may lead others to Salvation (Acts 16:24-30).
5. Keep praying because God is listening (Dan. 10:7-13).
6. Give thanks in every situation, knowing it is God's will for you (1 Thess. 5:16-18).
7. Finally, we must always be mindful that He will cause everything to work out for our good (Rom. 8:28-39).

We will never be informed when our trials will begin, how long our trials will last, or how severe they will be. God is not obligated to inform us of any of these things. What we do know is that God orchestrates all of our trials, He is in complete control all the time, and He will never allow us to be tempted or tried beyond what we can handle (1 Cor. 10:13).

He is the ultimate loving, protecting, and providing Father who allows us to be tried only so that we might be develop the likeness of His Son, Jesus Christ. Is there any human father among us who doesn't want the very best for his children? How much more then will the God of love, who is love, want for His children? Thank God for His Holy Word, which is able to strengthen and encourage us in the midst of our storms. So let's all begin to praise God regardless of our circumstances and believe Him for what He said. God cannot lie and will fulfill His promises if we remain faithful. Remember, our trials are from God and for our good. Honor Him, and He will honor you (1 Sam. 2:30b).

Meditate on These Scriptures

> My son, do not despise the LORD'S discipline and do not resent His rebuke, because the LORD disciplines those He loves, as a father the son he delights in. (Prov. 3:11-12 NIV)

> If you endure chastening, God deals with you as with sons; for what son is there whom a father does not chasten? But if you are without chastening, of which all have become partakers, then you are illegitimate and not sons. Furthermore, we have had human fathers who corrected us, and we paid them respect. Shall we not much more readily be in subjection to the Father of spirits and live? For they indeed for a few days chastened us as seemed best to them, but He for our profit, that we may be partakers of His holiness. Now no chastening seems to be joyful for the present, but painful; nevertheless, afterward it yields the peaceable fruit of righteousness to those who have been trained by it. (Heb. 12:7-11 NKJV)

Commit to Memory

Psalm 19:1: ***The heavens declare the glory of God; the skies proclaim the work of His hands.*** **(NIV)**

28

Why Do Some Christians Have to Suffer?

The concept of suffering is definitely synonymous with Christianity. An extensive study of Scripture will reveal that every powerful man or woman of God in the Bible has suffered at some point in his or her lifetime. Some of us may ask, "If Jesus Christ has already paid the penalty for our sins, why do we have to suffer?" If you've reached this chapter then you should already know the answer to that question, however, if for some reason you have skipped the previous chapters, then the answer is forthcoming. We live in a fallen world that is governed by the devil, and he hates Christians. He will do all he can to cause us to suffer. However, he is not in control of our lives. God is, and He has a purpose for our suffering.

Once we've been born again (accepted Jesus Christ into our lives as our Lord and Savior), God allows trials in our lives to develop and prepare us for service. This is not at all unfamiliar to us because every Christian knows that we will all experience trials; however, suffering is a little different. Suffering doesn't necessarily have to be a physical ailment or sickness, and it can last for an extended period of time. Trials generally last for a period or a season, and then God moves us on. In most cases suffering lasts longer and is far more severe than any trial we may experience. God reserves suffering for those He intends on using mightily. Although we may know someone who has suffered, our best examples will always come from the Bible.

Job and Joseph experienced severe trials and suffering far greater than what many of us will ever have to endure (Job 1:11-12; 2:7; Gen. 37:23-28; 39:19-20). Note that Joseph was seventeen years old when he was sold into slavery (Gen. 37:2, 23-28); he was thirty years of age when appointed over Egypt (Gen. 41:46). Jesus Christ suffered, and every one of the His disciples suffered, dying by crucifixion, beheading, and other horrible means (excluding John, who died of old age [John 21:15-24]). It is uncertain how Matthias died, but some say he was crucified and others believe he was stoned (he was the disciple chosen by the eleven remaining to replace Judas [Acts 1:23, 26]).

Those of us whom God allows to suffer must learn to respond correctly while suffering so that we can receive the required experience necessary to serve God in the capacity that He desires for us. The lessons we learn from suffering will prepare us for the exact purpose He created us for. Suffering will remove all sensitivity, immaturity, inexperience, and any hint of pride that we may have struggled with in the past. God's process of preparation will remove all of these ill and useless vices from our lives permanently (even when our flesh has the desire, the Holy Spirit will strengthen us in victory).

In most cases we will not understand what God is doing or why, but if He chooses to use us mightily it will definitely be because we know Him and have placed all of our faith in Him and Him alone (not our own abilities or success). When He chooses us, it also means that we have passed His heart test. He examined the true intentions of our heart, and it is acceptable in His sight (Job 1:6-8). Those whom He chooses generally have two things in common: they trust Him totally, and they obey Him regardless of the circumstances. Everyone in the Bible that He chose displayed an unshakable faith in Him, combined with an intense desire to live a life pleasing to Him (Gen. 39:2-9, 40; Job 13:15; 19:25; Matt. 26:36-39; Phil. 2:5-8).

These statements become more evident as we examine the lives of those whom God chose to use. Joseph's interpretation of the two dreams demonstrated his relationship with God and his faith in Him even in the midst of his suffering (Gen 40:8-19); Job's wife suggested he curse God and die, but Job held firm to his faith and obedience (Job 2:6-10); the apostle Paul suffered tremendously yet held fast to his faith in God (2 Cor. 11:22-31); and the life of Jesus Christ was a life of sacrifice, suffering, and total obedience to God the Father—even unto death (Phil. 2:6-11). These were all shining examples of suffering servants whose lives God chose to use mightily.

Often I have personally spoken with Christians who say that they want to be used mightily by God, yet few really know what that means. I'm not saying that they don't have the desire to serve. I just don't believe they understand the preparation that it takes, combined with that desire to be used mightily by God. I give all thanks and praise to God because He knows far better than we do what our true capabilities are and grants our prayers and requests accordingly. Our heavenly Father knows each of us personally and has already chosen the path that He desires for us in this journey called life.

Without God's preparation we would never be able to carry out the mighty works that He desires, because those works could not be achieved any other way. A broken spirit is a mighty tool in the hands of the LORD. The humility, patience, and perseverance that result from suffering cannot be taught in seminary or acquired any other way. Speaking of Himself, the Lord said, "Most assuredly, I say to you, unless a grain of wheat falls into the ground and dies, it remains alone; but if it dies it produces much grain" (John 12:24 NKJV). If the Lord had not suffered in death on our behalf, He could not have produced life for us. Just as the Lord's death produced life for us, our suffering and death to self will produce new life in us.

If we are among those whom God calls, our suffering will prepare us for leadership and enable us to help and even shepherd others in distress. Joseph's suffering prepared him for leadership over all of Egypt (as second in command) and to save his father's household in the midst of difficult times (Gen. 41:37-40; 45:5, 7-8), the apostle Paul's experiences gained through suffering prepared him to author thirteen books in the Bible (some believe he also wrote Hebrews), the suffering of our Lord and Savior Jesus Christ enabled Him to identify with us and help us when we're suffering (Heb. 2:17-18; 4:14-16).

Take heed to the lives and experiences of those whom God has allowed to suffer, and make note of their responses in these challenging circumstances. They serve as our examples for life and service. Remember that God allows suffering for our good; in fact, He allows suffering for greatness. So if you believe that God is allowing you to suffer, it's because He desires for you to be great. Also keep in mind that God reserves suffering for those whom He entrusts a great work. "For I consider that the sufferings of this present time are not worthy to be compared with the glory which shall be revealed in us" (Rom. 8:18 NKJV), Paul wrote.

Those whom the LORD loves He chastens, and those whom He uses mightily he allows to suffer. Hold fast and continue to trust God if you experience suffering, and He will exalt you in due season. God is faithful!

Meditate on These Scriptures

And who is he who will harm you if you become followers of what is good? But even if you should suffer for righteousness' sake, you are blessed. "And do not be afraid of their threats, nor be troubled." But sanctify the Lord God in your hearts, and always be ready to give a defense to everyone who asks you a reason for the hope that is in you, with meekness and fear; having a good conscience, that when they defame you as evil doers, those who revile your good conduct in Christ may be ashamed. For it is better, if it is the will of God, to suffer for doing good than for doing evil. (1 Pet. 2:13-17 NKJV)

For I consider that the sufferings of this present time are not worthy to be compared with the glory which shall be revealed in us. For the earnest expectation of the creation eagerly waits for the revealing of the sons of God. For the creation was subject to futility, not willingly, but because of Him who subjected it in hope; because the creation itself also will be delivered from the bondage of corruption into the glorious liberty of the children of God. (Rom. 8:18-21 NKJV)

Commit to Memory

Hebrews 2:18: ***Because He Himself suffered when He was tempted, He is able to help those who are being tempted.*** **(NIV)**

29

Where Are You Storing Your Treasures?

Many of us spend large segments of our time worrying about our future. We make all sorts of plans for our retirement and put little emphasis on our eternal destination. Because life is short, death is inevitable, and eternity is everlasting, we must reevaluate our plans for the future. We must begin to believe God regarding our future plans and let go of all anxiety about how we will survive later in life (Matt. 6:25-33). This does not mean that we should not take the necessary steps to provide for our future and the future of our loved ones. This simply means that no Christian should suffer from anxiety attacks regarding his/her future.

After we've consulted God in regard to finding the most qualified professionals to advise us about making provision (wise investments) for the future, prayer combined with our faith will comfort us in Christ Jesus (Phil. 4:6-7). The Lord grants each of us the gift of His peace, which is unlike the peace that the world offers. The peace that comes from the Lord promotes comfort and expels all fear; the world offers a false sense of peace that cannot be relied on because the devil governs it and he is the father of all lies (John 8:41-44; 2 Cor. 4:3-4). Our trust can only rest in Him who cannot lie.

Every investment we make on earth is at risk. It can be lost, stolen, or even destroyed; but unlike any man-made system, only God has the ability to safely keep all that we entrust to Him (Matt. 6:19-21; 2 Tim. 1:12). Because we live in a fallen world dominated by greed, our economic future will always be unstable. Many of our present investments will not have the value that we expected when the day comes to cash in. God, however, is faithful. He will keep all that we entrust to Him. God is able to protect what we have from the devourer who seeks to steal and destroy all that we acquire (Mal. 3:11; John 10:10).

Trusting God with the welfare of our future means walking in obedience to His Word, acknowledging Him first in all that we do (that means praying and seeking God before we make our final decision [Prov. 3:5-6]), and exercising extreme patience when waiting to hear from Him (God is not obligated to answer us immediately—His time is not like ours [2 Pet. 3:8]). These three principles are very important because most of our personal catastrophes occur when we act in disobedience to God (at that time we are fare play for the enemy, Satan) and make decisions based solely on our own opinions and personal experiences as a result of our lack of faith and debilitating anxiety.

The reason we must trust God is simple. The entire earth and everything in it belongs to Him (Ps. 24:1-2). He knows the past, present, and future. No stockbroker or investment banker can make those claims (at least not regarding the future and to some extent the present also). Most importantly God loves us more than anyone is capable of loving us, and He wants the very best for us. Who can question the love of God after He gave His only begotten Son for the sake of all mankind (John 3:16-17)? Here are three principles regarding our heritage from which we can continuously draw confidence.

1. God determines our future (Acts 17:26-28; James 4:13-15).
2. God will supply all our needs (Phil. 4:19).
3. The foolish invest in the world, but the wise invest in God (Luke 12:13-21).
4. Our inheritance through Jesus Christ is stored in heaven (1 Pet. 1:3-5).
5. He causes all things to work out for us (Rom. 8:28).

Although we are presently living on earth, our permanent home is in heaven. Our natural life is short, but our spiritual life is everlasting (Luke 16:19-26; 2 Cor. 5:8; Phil 1:21-23; 1 Thess. 4:16-17). For this reason we must place most of our emphasis and all of our focus on our eternal home and not on our present earthly existence and residence. We must change our present way of thinking and begin to focus on spiritual things—the things that matter to God. Focusing on spiritual things will help us to put our life, both spiritual and natural, into proper perspective. Here are some Scriptures that are helpful when prioritizing our lives.

1. We are not at home here on earth (Phil. 3:18-21).
2. Our natural life is short (Job 14:1-5).
3. God's Word promises eternal life to those who believe (John 5:24).
4. Work in God's harvest so you can reap heavenly rewards (John 4:36-38).

None of this means that we shouldn't make an attempt to save for our future. It simply means that our primary focus should be on eternity and not on retirement. Place your future plans in the hand of God, and he will provide for your retirement and eternity. Trust Him and watch how He gives freely all things to those who belong to Him.

1. Don't worry over things you truly cannot control (Luke 12:22-34).
2. Seek first the kingdom of God and his righteousness, and He will supply all that we need (Matt. 6:30-34).
3. Obedience to God will secure your future and your possessions (Matt. 7:24-27).
4. Focus on wealth with God and not the world (Luke 12:13-21).
5. God will not withhold anything from us (Rom. 8:32).

Meditate on These Scriptures

Keep falsehood and lies far from me; give me neither poverty nor riches, but give me only my daily bread. Otherwise, I may have too much and disown you and say, "Who is the LORD? Or I may become poor and steal, and so dishonor the name of my God. (Prov. 30:8-9 NIV)

"Again the kingdom of heaven is like a dragnet that was cast into the sea and gathered some of every kind, which, when it was full, they drew to shore; and they sat down and gathered the good into vessels, but threw the bad away. So it will be at the end of the age. The angels will come forth, separate the wicked from among the just, and cast them into the furnace of fire. There will be wailing and gnashing of teeth." (Matt. 13:47-50 NKJV)

Commit to Memory

1 Timothy 6:7: ***For we brought nothing into this world, and it is certain we can carry nothing out.***

30

Who's Blocking Your Blessings?

How many times have you heard or used the term "blessing blocker(s)"? Often we use this term when we refer to people we believe Satan uses to interfere with the plans that God has established for our lives. We characterize them as the tools Satan uses to distract us, to frustrate us, or to quench our spiritual desires or plans. To the surprise of many of us, these so called "blessing blockers" are closer than we know—they are none other than ourselves. It may seem ridiculous, but the phrase, "You are your own worst enemy," is one that we have to begin to take very seriously.

There is no need for the devil to place anyone in our path to block our blessings because we do an excellent job ourselves. Disobedience is the number one obstacle that prevents us from being blessed, with pride and an unforgiving heart following closely behind. The prophet Samuel compared disobedience to witchcraft (1 Sam. 15:22-23). Pride will lead us to destruction (Prov. 16:18), and an unforgiving heart will prevent us from receiving forgiveness from the God of our salvation (Matt. 6:14-15). Here are some questions I think we should ask ourselves when we believe we are no longer being blessed.

- Do you choose life and obey the Word of God, or do you choose death (Deut. 30:11-20)?
- Do you do the good that you know to do (Prov. 3:27-28; James 4:17)?
- Are you trusting and seeking God regarding your decisions (Prov. 3:5-6)?
- Are you making disciples (Matt. 28:18-20)?

God simply cannot bless us if we are living in sin. Too often we try to fool ourselves by believing that what we're doing isn't that bad, but all sin is bad and separates us from our heavenly Father (Isa. 59:1-2). We also must be mindful that as Christians the most important communication line in our lives is our prayer line, our direct access to God. If we harbor any sort of sin in our lives, that communication line to God goes dead (Ps. 66:18). We can't call the phone company to repair this situation. We must repent and confess our sin to God. Once we've confessed our sins, God will reopen our line of communication to Him.

Nothing is more important than our ability to communicate with our heavenly Father. Once we've begun to understand this very important fact, we will be more conscious to make sure that we make every attempt to remove anything from our lives that in any way could possibly hinder our relationship and ability to communicate with God. In some cases (a very few) our ignorance is the cause of the disruption of our ability to communicate with God (Hos. 4:6). Unfortunately, we don't get any pity from God (and we certainly don't deserves any) for being ignorant of His commands and desires of us.

We are presently living in the greatest time in history known to mankind. We have a vast amount of information (Christian information) that is available to us through print, TV, and the World Wide Web.

All of these things pale in comparison to the breathtaking facts that we have God's own Spirit living inside of us (John 14:15-18), that Jesus Christ is seated at the right hand of the Father interceding on behalf of every one of us (Rom. 8:34), and that we are presently in the dispensation (age) of grace (Eph. 2:1-10). If we cannot succeed at this point, it is no one's fault but our own. Here is a short list of important facts we must be mindful of regarding any form of sin that we may believe is hidden from God (not confessed or repented).

- Our sins will always be exposed because we can't hide from God. (Ps. 139:8-12).
- Regardless of how slick we think we are, God can't be fooled (Gal. 6:7-8).
- Every living thing is exposed before God (Heb. 4:13).

It is plain to see that no one can block our blessings (not even Satan). We must begin to walk in obedience to the Word of God and remove those devices or people from the place in our lives that belongs to God. If we believe an associate (friend or family member) is causing us to fall away from the faith and refuses to turn from his/her sinful ways, we must take action and make a change (Prov. 13:20; 1 Cor. 15:33). If we feel that there is something in our lives that is causing us to fall away from God, we must make every attempt to remove it from our lives; and if we don't believe that we have the strength to do it alone, we must seek out a strong Christian brother or sister whom we know very well (we must know them personally; 1 John 4:1) and pray continually with them for God's grace to succeed (James 5:13-18).

We know that God is a jealous God and will not be second in the life of any Christian (Deut. 20:3-5; Luke 14:26-27). He loves us too much to allow us to follow something or someone that will ultimately cause us to be destroyed. God has granted us free will (limited) and does not control every moment of our lives; however, He encamps His angels around us to protect us (Ps. 34:7; 37:23; Jer. 10:23) and places His Holy Spirit inside of us to teach us and direct our paths. As we begin to allow God to transform our previous way of thinking, let's take notice of five important facts about our present relationship with God.

1. Have you put God on the back burner (Rev. 2:1-5; note; "first works" [cf. Deut. 6:5])?
2. Is God still the joy of your life (Ps. 37:4-5)?
3. Have you turned from righteousness and returned to the world (2 Pet. 2:20-22)?
4. Obedience is the key to our blessings (Isa. 1:11-20).
5. Return to your first love (Rev. 2:1-7).

We must always be mindful that only we are responsible for the outcome of our lives and no one else. When we return to God and begin to put Him first in our lives, He will not disappoint us (1 Sam. 2:30).

Meditate on These Scriptures

> Blessed is everyone who fears the LORD, who walks in His ways. When you eat the labor of your hands, you shall be happy, and it shall be well with you. Your wife shall be like a fruitful vine in the very heart of your house, your children like olive plants all around your table. Behold, thus shall the man be blessed who fears the LORD. The LORD bless you out of Zion, and may you see your children's children. Peace be upon Israel! (Ps. 128 NKJV)

> Behold, how good and how pleasant it is for brethren to dwell together in unity! It is like the precious

ointment upon the head, that ran down upon the beard, even Aaron's beard: that went down to the skirts of his garments; as the dew of Hermon, and as the dew that descended upon the mountains of Zion: for there the LORD commanded His blessings, even life forevermore. (Ps. 133 KJV)

Commit to Memory

Romans 6:23: ***For the wages of sin is death, but the gift of God is eternal life in Christ Jesus our Lord.*** **(NKJV)**

31

Access to God Through Christ

Of all the topics I've read and all the material I've written, this is, in my opinion, the most important to God's children—access to God through Jesus Christ. Take a moment and think about these questions. When you were a child and desired something of or from one of your parents, did you take your request to them, or did you ask a friend to take your request to them? I'm certain you didn't do the latter. So why do so many of us expect someone else (pastor, deacon, elder, parent, grandparent, etc) to pray to God for us? Please don't misunderstand this statement.

We definitely should be praying for each other on a daily basis. The Bible clearly teaches this important principle (John 17:20; Eph. 1:15-16; Phil. 1:4; James 5:16-18, and many more). However, we should not undervalue the importance of entering God's awesome presence on our own behalf by relying on someone else to pray for us. Praying to God is a very important part of developing our relationship with Him. The more we pray to God, the more we will learn to trust and obey Him. Our continuous prayers mean we believe or else we wouldn't pray. We pray because we believe He hears and answers our requests and petitions.

This is obedience to the Lord (Matt. 26:41; 2 Thess. 3:1-2; 1 Tim. 2:1-4). We should pray for others because the Bible says so! Praying for others shows that we have compassion for the welfare of people and true concern for the eternal destination of their souls. However, the wonderful sacrifice of our Lord has enabled us to go before His Father's presence (providing we are living in obedience; see Ps. 66:18) on our own behalf without the need of intercession from any other human.

We must understand the finished work of Jesus Christ and the Old Testament history of intercessory prayer to realize the true importance of access to God the Father through Jesus Christ our Lord.

The Sin of Adam and Eve Separated All of Mankind from God

In the beginning man's relationship with God was a wonderful bond void of any sort of separation. God loved man and communicated with him plainly and clearly without any division between Him and His creation (Gen. 1:27-31; 2:15-23). Man's disobedience was devastating to his relationship with God. This act of total disobedience to God's command (Gen. 2:17) formed a gap between God and man that only Jesus Christ could close (Gen. 3:23-24). The promise of the Savior through the seed of the woman would be God's answer to a redemption plan that would repair the relationship between Him and the entire human race (Gen. 3:14-15).

As a result of the fall (human disobedience), man would be required to make offerings and sacrifices to the LORD (Gen. 4:1-4; 8:20-21; Leviticus 1-7). The first noted sacrifice for mankind occurred in Genesis 3:21, as God sacrificed the life of an animal to make a covering out of skin for Adam and Eve. This would signify generations of animal sacrifices as the (covering) atonement for sin. God began to use His prophets and priests to intercede on behalf of all of mankind (Gen. 20:7, 17-18; Exod. 32:30-35; Josh. 7:1-26; 1 Sam. 7:1-10; Job 42:7-8)—only they could enter into God's presence to atone for the sins of the people.

When the Old Testament priest interceded on behalf of the people, he would go behind a curtain known as a veil. Only the high priest could go behind the veil to offer sacrifices for the sins of the people (Exod. 26:31-33). Because of the finished work (sacrifice) of Jesus Christ, the penalty for sin has been paid in full and the veil between God and all of mankind has been removed permanently (Matt. 27:27-56; John 19:30). We can now enter into God's holy presence without an earthly intercessor through our Lord and Savior Jesus Christ.

- The Lord performed the final act of sacrifice for mankind (Isaiah 53; 1 Pet. 2:21-25) and
- is now seated at the right hand of God the Father, interceding on our behalf (Rom. 8:34; 1 Tim. 2:5).
- Jesus Christ is the ultimate high priest with a ministry of eternal intercession for all who call on Him (Heb. 7:20-28).
- Because we serve the most high priest and Mediator between God and all mankind, we do not need any human being to intercede for us (Heb. 8:1-6). He is the perfect intercessor.
- The Lord has also left a comforter to help us, even as we pray (Rom. 8:26-27).
- The teaching ministry of the Holy Spirit will enable us to understand the importance of entering God's presence on our own behalf (John 14:26).

- Waiting on someone else to pray on our behalf is an act of disobedience and a lack of faith in God's promises (Matt. 7:7-11; John 14:12-14).

We no longer need to seek the priest or the pastor or anyone else to pray for us. Jesus Christ paid the full penalty for sin, thus enabling those who confess and believe that He is Lord to enter the presence of God Almighty when they pray. Because of the awesome price that the Lord paid on our behalf, it is imperative that we take full advantage of our access to the Father through Him. God desires for us to come directly to Him with our heart-emptying prayers because He cares for us. The Spirit of the Lord spoke through the apostle Peter and said, "Casting all your care upon Him, for He cares for you" (1 Pet. 5:7).

The Lord also promised that if we cast our cares on Him, He will not allow us to be overtaken (Ps. 55:22). We must take this opportunity to accept this wonderful invitation and begin to pray daily on our own behalf and allow God to fulfill His promises in us and through us. Our access to God is a wonderful picture of His loving grace. Because He truly loves every one of us, His desire is to fellowship with each of us on a person level. He expects us to come to Him with our problems, prayers, and petitions. Even our Lord offered Himself freely to us, inviting us to yoke up with Him and promising that He would help us and lighten our burdens (Matt. 11:28-30).

If you haven't taken advantage of this wonderful grace that God has made available to all who accept His Son, start today. If your heart is clean, enter God's presence on your own behalf and allow God through His Spirit to strengthen your relationship with Him. Thank God for His grace, which welcomes all who love Him to enter His holy place and fellowship with Him. I pray that you take advantage of this great opportunity because He is waiting for you. God bless you. Please take notice to the definition for veil; I think it is very important that we understand what it means.

Veil – "a curtain in the tabernacle or Temple that separated the Holy Place from the Holy of Holies (or most Holy Place). Only the priest could go behind the veil, and this occurred only one day each year—on the Day of Atonement (Lev. 16:2). But when Jesus died on the cross, 'the veil of the temple was torn in two from top to bottom' (Matt. 27:51), showing that Jesus had opened a new and living way into the presence of God through His death (Heb. 6:19; 9:3)" *(Nelson's Illustrated Dictionary of the Bible).*

Meditate on These Scriptures

> And we have such trust through Christ toward God. Not that we are sufficient of ourselves to think of anything as being from ourselves, but our sufficiency is from God, who has made us sufficient as ministers of the new covenant, not of the letter but of the Spirit; for the letter kills but the Spirit gives life. (2 Cor. 3:4-6 NKJV)

> This is the confidence we have in approaching God: that if we ask anything according to His will, He hears us. And if we know He hears us—whatever we ask—we know that we have what we ask of Him. (1 John 5:14-15 NIV)

Commit to Memory

1 Timothy 2:5: ***For there is one God and one Mediator between God and men, the man Christ Jesus.*** **(NKJV)**

32

The Power Of Love

The Bible says, "Where faith, hope, and love abide—love is the greatest" (1 Cor. 13:13). The Bible also says, "Love covers a multitude of sins" (1 Pet. 4:8). Jesus said the second greatest commandment was to love your neighbor as yourself (Matt. 22:36-40). It's not by coincidence that the two greatest commands involved love—loving God and loving one's neighbor. Love is important to God because He is love. He personifies everything that defines love. It was His great love that inspired our creation (His desire for an intimate fellowship with mankind), and it was His love that delivered the human race from eternal damnation (John 3:16).

To understand love and what it really means, we must first understand that there are various types of love (but only one true love). Here are some definitions that will help us to better understand this powerful force that has the ability to save, heal, and impact so many.

Love – "Unselfish, loyal, and benevolent concern for the well being of another" *(Holman Bible Dictionary).*

***Phileo* Love** – *Phileo* is the Greek word for love that is found in the word *Philadelphia,* which means, "love of brother"*(Holman Bible Dictionary).* The natural man typically displays this type of love. This is the world's love, and it's activated by what it receives. For example, I love you as long as you supply my needs, whatever they may be (money, sex, shelter, etc). In contrast to the world's view of brotherly love, our love should exemplify true concern for the well-being of others.

***Agape* Love** – Agape is a Greek word that describes the nature of the love of God toward His beloved Son (John 17:26), toward the human race generally (John 3:16; Rom. 5:8), and toward those who believe on the Lord Jesus Christ (John 14:21) *(Nelson's Illustrated Dictionary of the Bible).*

***Eros* Love – "sexual** love or desire" *(Webster's New World Dictionary and Thesaurus).* This love is based on sexual desire (lust) only and is more of a physical feeling or attraction than real love. The English word *erotic* is derived from the Greek word *eros.*

Note that the word ***charity*** comes from the Latin word *caritas,* which means "dearness," "affection," or "high regard." Some Bible versions frequently use this word to translate the Greek words for love (1 Cor. 8:1; Col. 3:14; 1 Thess. 3:6; 1 Tim. 1:5; 1 Pet. 4:8).

The Bible is clear in regard to what love really is. We generally equate love to just a feeling or strong emotion, but the Bible teaches us that love is far more than that. It teaches us that love is patient, kind, forgiving, giving, and much more. Take notice of the way the Bible portrays love in comparison to how we generally view love.

1. What is love (1 Cor. 13:4-8)?
2. Love is the fruit of the Spirit (Gal. 5:22-23).
3. Love binds all things together in perfect unity (Col. 3:12-14).
4. Love forgives one another (1 Pet. 4:8).

The power of love will enable us to give to others without concern for what we will receive in return and to forgive others in situations we normally couldn't. It also shows mercy toward others (1 Pet. 4:8), something that the loveless heart is not capable of doing. These acts are not natural to those who do not have the Spirit of God living inside them. By nature the natural man will repay evil for evil, but God's desire is for us to forgive (Matt. 5:38-42) and to allow Him to execute vengeance upon the wicked (Rom. 12:17-21).

In today's society (the world in general) people use the word *love* so often and so loosely that it seems to have lost its power. In fact, most people don't even understand the meaning of the word. Love is a verb, which denotes action. It doesn't necessarily relate to sexual intimacy. You cannot love someone yet have no desire to do something for that person unless he or she gives you something or does something for you in return—that's not love at all. Love wants to share and do for another, love is considerate, kind, and everything that makes life worthwhile. Here are some more very good examples of how the power of love should impact the lives of every Christian.

- If we really love the Lord, we will be obedient (John 14:15, 21).
- Do we love our parents and children (Eph. 6:1-4)?
- If love abides in us, we will help our neighbor (Luke 10:30-37).

To have *agape* love for someone is to have an unconditional love for that person that cannot be easily shaken (regardless of what happens). This is the kind of love God expects us (Christians) to have for one another (John 15:12). The Lord told His disciples the meaning of love and later exemplified it with His own sacrifice (John 15:13). This love shouldn't be a challenge for spouses, siblings, parents, or children. Unfortunately, because we are living in the last days, very few households represent true *agape* love. Today, just as many Christian marriages end in divorce as in the world, and our families are filled with dark secrets (incest, abuse, jealousy, etc.).

We must start today and break the old cycle of harboring animosity and allow the Holy Spirit to fill our hearts with the love of God. That is the only way we can learn to love those who have hurt or abandoned us at some point in our lives. If we do not allow God's Spirit to soften our hardened hearts so that we can learn to forgive and love, we will be in danger of missing out on God's promise (Matt. 6:14-15). We cannot receive forgiveness for our sins if we are not willing to forgive others—that is the whole concept of grace and salvation. Turn from the past today, and allow the power of God's love to transform your life.

We must begin to pray daily that the God of our salvation will soften our hardened hearts and enable us to live lives of love that are pleasing to Him.

Meditate on These Scriptures

> Owe no one anything except to love one another, for he who loves another has fulfilled the law. For the commandments, "You shall not commit adultery," "You shall not murder," "You shall not steal," "You shall not bear false witness," "You shall not covet," and if there is any other commandment, are all

summed up in this saying, namely, "You shall love your neighbor as yourself." Love does no harm to a neighbor; therefore love is the fulfillment of the law. (Rom. 13:8-10 NKJV)

Love suffers long and is kind; love does not envy; love does not parade itself, is not puffed up; does not behave rudely; does not seek its own, is not provoked, thinks no evil; does not rejoice in iniquity, but rejoices in the truth; bears all things, believes all things, hopes all things, endures all things. Love never fails. But whether there are prophecies, they will fail; whether there are tongues, they will cease; whether there is knowledge, it will vanish away. (1 Cor. 13:4-8 NKJV)

And now abide faith, hope, love, these three; but the greatest is love. (1 Cor. 13:13 NKJV)

Commit to Memory

John 15:13: ***"Greater love have no one than this, than to lay down one's life for his friends."*** **(NKJV)**

Conclusion

This publication may not answer all of your questions or solve all your problems. It is simply a tool that will enable you to better understand the Bible and how to apply the principles of Scripture to your everyday life. I believe a daily dose of the Word of God is essential for everyone, regardless of what office you hold in your church or ministry. The topics covered in this publication are a result of my experiences in ministry and my years of studying the Bible.

Nothing is more important than getting to know God, the Creator of the universe and all things that exist. The catch is that you will only get to know Him by reading and studying the Bible. The unfortunate truth is that most of us prefer to do just about everything else but read the Bible. However, if we would just begin to read God's Word on a daily basis, His Holy Spirit will enlighten us and reveal Him to us in ways that we never could have imagined. The Bible says, "Oh, taste and see that the LORD is good; blessed is the man who trust in Him!" (Ps. 34:8). Once you establish a relationship with God, you will not be disappointed.

The Word of God can comfort us when we're in pain, it can encourage us when we're lacking confidence, it can offer hope in times of despair, it can build awesome inner strength, and it will develop wisdom and knowledge like nothing or no one else can. The Bible is the only book known to mankind that can offer so much. So why don't more people dedicate their personal time reading the Bible? First, they truly don't know what they're missing. Second, they believe they have more important things to do. Third, they think attending church on Sunday and hearing a twenty-five- to thirty-minute sermon is sufficient.

Finally, they are totally blinded by the adversary. He uses the same old subtle tricks he's been using for hundreds of years, namely, distraction, procrastination, and lies—Distraction: "I'm too busy"; procrastination: "I'll do it later"; and lies: "I went to church Sunday, so I'm good until next Sunday." It's funny, but we wouldn't treat anyone but God this way. We make time for everyone and everything else but God, the most important person in our lives. God is not human, but He is alive and can be grieved and made jealous (Josh. 24:19-20; Eph. 4:30).

Once you begin to study God's Word on a daily basis, He will transform your mind in ways you could not have even dreamed of. Give your life totally to the LORD; He has already given His Son's life for ours. My beloved friends, I bid you Godspeed.

SOURCES CITED

Agnes, Michael, ed. *Webster's New World Dictionary and Thesaurus,* 2nd ed. (Cleveland: Wiley Publishing, 2002).

Butler, Trent C., ed. *Holman Bible Dictionary* (Nashville: Holman Bible Publishers, 1991).

Lockyer, Herbert, Sr., F. F. Bruce, and R.K. Harrison, eds. *Nelson's Illustrated Dictionary of the Bible* (Nashville: Thomas Nelson Publishers, 1986).

Strong, James. *The New Strong's Expanded Dictionary Of Bible Words* (Nashville: Thomas Nelson Publishers, 2001).

Walvoord, John F., and Roy B. Zuck, eds., *Bible Knowledge Commentary (New Testament)* (Colorado Springs: Chariot Victor Publishing, 1983).

Suggested resources For Spiritual Growth

Humility, ed. Andrew Murray, D.D., CLC Publications, ISBN 0-87508-710-8

Holman Bible Dictionary, ed. Trent C. Butler, Holman Bible Publishers, ISBN 1-55819-053-8

Nelson's Illustrated Bible Dictionary, ed. Herbert Lockyer, Thomas Nelson Publishing ISBN 07852-5051-4

Strong's Exhausted Concordance Of The Bible, ed. James Strong, Hendrickson Publishers ISBN 0-917006-01-1

The Bible for everyday Life, ed. George Carey, William B. Eerdmans Publishing Co. (2nd edit) ISBN 0-8028-4157-0

The Interpreter's One – Volume Commentary Of The Bible, ed. Charles M. Laymon, Abingdon Press ISBN 0-687-19299-4

The Bible Knowledge Commentary, ed. John F. Walvoord & Roy B. Zuck
Chariot Victor Publishing ISBN 0-88207-813-5
(Old Testament.)
0-88207-812-7 (New Testament.)

The Bible Promise Book (KJV), Barbour Publishing
ISBN 1-55748-105-9
The Bible Promise Book (NIV), Barbour Publishing
ISBN1-55748-235-7

The Holy Spirit, ed. Bill Bright, New Life Publications
ISBN 0-86605-158-9

The New Strong's Expanded Dictionary of Bible Words, ed. James Strong, Thomas Nelson publishers
ISBN 0-7852-4676-2

Tortured For Christ, ed. Pastor Richard Wurmbrand, living Sacrifice Book Company
ISBN 0-88264-326-6

The Pursuit of GOD, ed. A.W. Tozer, Christian Publications Inc. ISBN 0-87509-366-3

Breinigsville, PA USA
06 June 2010
239317BV00001B/4/P